Inclusion in the City

Selection, schooling and community

Edited by Patricia Potts

RoutledgeFalmer
Taylor & Francis Group

LONDON AND NEW YORK

First published 2003
by RoutledgeFalmer
11 New Fetter Lane, London EC4P 4EE

Simultaneously published in the USA and Canada
by RoutledgeFalmer
29 West 35th Street, New York, NY 10001

RoutledgeFalmer is an imprint of the Taylor & Francis Group

© 2003 Patricia Potts

Typeset in Sabon by
Keystroke, Jacaranda Lodge, Wolverhampton
Printed and bound in Great Britain by
St Edmundsbury Press, Bury St Edmunds, Suffolk

British Library Cataloguing in Publication Data
A catalogue record for this book is available from the British Library

Library of Congress Cataloging in Publication Data
A catalog record has been requested

ISBN 0–415–26803–6 (hbk)
ISBN 0–415–26804–4 (pbk)

Inclusion in the City

How can policies for inclusion in education be coherent and sustainable? Why is geography crucial to the development of inclusive educational communities?

Inclusion in the City explores inclusion and exclusion in the context of policy and practice in one English city – Birmingham. Here, a commitment to redressing the inequalities experienced by many learners has been inhibited by difficulty in securing agreement to a definite policy for inclusion and, consequently, in sustaining initiatives for strengthening participation in community comprehensive education.

Grounded in an understanding of inclusion as a political and moral project, the book presents a range of perspectives from policymakers and practitioners. Detailed case studies, based on research specially undertaken for this book, relate inclusion to key issues in contemporary education:

- The effects of selection by attainment
- Faith schools and their communities
- Single-sex education and inclusive schools
- Participation in further education
- Social mobility

Insightful, thought-provoking and original, *Inclusion in the City* detaches processes of inclusion and exclusion from the language of special needs, connecting them instead to the language of educational reform. In so doing it highlights links between participation in education and poverty, gender and cultural background, as well as the absence of a link between urban and educational renewal.

Work on this book was supported by a grant from the Barrow Cadbury Trust.

Patricia Potts is Senior Research Fellow at Canterbury Christ Church University College.

Contents

Illustrations

Contributors

Tony Booth, Professor of Inclusive and International Education, Centre for Educational Research, Canterbury Christ Church University College

Gwenn Edwards, learning mentor, Co-educational Community Secondary School, Birmingham

Patricia Potts, Senior Research Fellow, Centre for Educational Research, Canterbury Christ Church University College

Sharon Rustemier, freelance education writer and researcher

Preface

Members of our research team have been visiting Birmingham since 1997, and this book represents an extended collaboration.

Our approach is underpinned by Tony Booth's analysis of processes of inclusion and exclusion, and he co-directed the team's research activities. Concepts of and contexts for inclusion/exclusion are many-layered and their examination reveals dilemmas that cannot necessarily be resolved. Moving towards coherent policies for participation in education requires political and ethical commitment to a project of comprehensive reform.

The project was carried out during a particular period, and the stories we have collected and analysed represent experiences of the city that belong to these years. We raise and debate issues that emerged at the time of our involvement with colleagues and young people in Birmingham and, as we left to write up what we learned, the life of the city moved on. We argue, however, that the significance of these issues for the understanding of inclusion and exclusion endures.

In the contexts of primary, secondary and specialized schooling, as well as further education, we discuss faith schools, educational and urban renewal, gender discrepancies in attainment levels, student choice and the consequences of mobility for participation in education.

We were welcomed into the city, and we offer our book in return.

Acknowledgements

Our research was supported by the Barrow Cadbury Trust. We would like to thank its Director, Eric Adams, for his consistent support.

We thank all those who made us welcome in Birmingham over the years of the project. We appreciate their generosity and candour.

We are grateful to the administrators of the Centre for Educational Research at Canterbury Christ Church University College for their practical help.

Figures 2 and 3 are reproduced from Ordnance Survey mapping on behalf of The Controller of Her Majesty's Stationery Office © Crown Copyright. Licence Number MC 100039328.

Figure 4 © Jonathan Berg. www.bplphoto.co.uk
Figure 6 © Jonathan Berg. www.bplphoto.co.uk
Figure 5 © Gary Kirkham.

Chapter 1

Inclusion and exclusion in the city

Concepts and contexts

Tony Booth

In this chapter I introduce an approach to inclusion and exclusion. I adopt a broad view concerned with increasing the participation of all in education and society and in reducing all forms of discrimination and devaluation. I then briefly examine conceptions of inclusion within government policies. I indicate the extent to which such policies provide a coherent strategy for the development of education which acts as a resource for, or a barrier to, my version of inclusive educational development. This discussion provides a national context within which policies for inclusion in Birmingham are themselves developed as described in Chapter 2. A three-way comparison becomes possible. How should we define inclusion and exclusion? How is inclusion and exclusion conceived in government policy? How is inclusion and exclusion perceived in the city of Birmingham?

PUTTING BOUNDARIES AROUND INCLUSION AND EXCLUSION

Any attempt to deepen our understanding of inclusion and exclusion has to start from a definition of terms. Definitions can appear to interrupt the flow of a narrative, but they are important; if we simply go along with the variety of ways the terms are used we reproduce the inconsistencies and contradictions in such practice. The dominant view of inclusion in education continues to associate the term with disabled children or those otherwise categorized as having 'special educational needs'. In the 1986 Education Act, 'exclusion' was used to mean the suspension and expulsion from school of students seen to be in breach of disciplinary rules (DES 1986). Subsequently it became strongly associated with this use. However, since 1997, with the establishment of the Cabinet Office Social Exclusion Unit, the term 'social exclusion' has been used more broadly, to cover a range of social limitations on the participation of people, from poverty to reactions to teenage pregnancy. Discrimination against disabled people appears not to be seen as *social* exclusion, which might suggest that there are other forms of exclusion which are *natural*.

We see inclusion as concerned with reducing all exclusionary pressures in education and society, thus providing a dynamic relationship between the two concepts. We view inclusion in education as concerned with *increasing participation in, and reducing exclusion from, the learning opportunities, cultures and communities of the mainstream*. Inclusion is a never-ending process, working towards an ideal when all exclusionary pressures within education and society are removed. The identification of inclusion with an aspect of student identity such as an impairment or ethnicity is self-defeating since students are whole people with multiple, complex identities. When it is associated with a devaluing label, such as 'a child *with special educational needs*', it involves a particular contradiction. The inclusion in education of a child categorized as '*having special educational needs*' involves their de-categorization. Inclusion has to be connected to the recognition and appreciation of all aspects of diversity. Yet, arguments about the theoretical difficulties in approaching inclusion from a single issue should not be taken to diminish the need to counter devaluations of people because of their disability, class, gender, sexual orientation or ethnicity.

Our definition of inclusion contains further terms which themselves require examination. *Participation* in education involves going beyond *access*. It implies learning alongside others and collaborating with them in shared lessons. It involves active engagement with what is learnt and taught and having a say in how education is experienced. But participation also involves being recognized for oneself and being accepted for oneself: I participate with you when you recognize me as a person like yourself and accept me for who I am. We also need to see schools as a major source but not the only source of education within communities, which adds further intricacy to notions of participation in education. Education is wider than schooling. It is an activity in, for, and with communities.

The definition also introduces the concept of *culture*. Raymond Williams (1976) left a gift for those wrestling with the concept of 'culture' when he referred to it as 'one of the two or three most complicated words in the English language'. But we can begin to piece together important elements of a definition for education. Cultures can be seen as stable ways of life, shared between groups of people, which can be communicated across generations and contribute to the formation of identities. Cultures are established and expressed through language and values. Cultures involve explicit or implicit rules for identifying and responding to outsiders. Inclusive cultures encourage a recognition that a variety of ways of life and forms of identity can coexist and that communication between them is enriching.

Community is another elusive concept. Its intrinsic connection to education has been persuasively argued by Fielding (1999). Yet some deny its validity inside or outside education (Barber 1996). It is as if the blood family has become, for such people, the only grouping to which individuals can have a sentimental attachment. This may be politically or economically convenient, but it is a denial of reality. People form a whole variety of networks, narrow and extended, based on common interests. Real families frequently blend into a wider circle of friends and acquaintances. Social policies, including education policy, can either reinforce or disrupt the building of communities. Communities and cultures are mutually sustaining. An inclusive education is concerned with the creation and sustenance of communities within and outside schools.

A deep view of participation and the development of inclusive cultures require a transformational rather than an assimilationist view of inclusion. On an assimilationist view students and staff are expected to fit into exclusive cultures embodying restricted notions of normality. Curricula, teaching approaches and views of achievement are seen as fixed and failure for many is guaranteed. A transformative view starts from a recognition of diversity amongst students and sees it as a rich resource for learning. There is no single standard of achievement. Schools adapt to the identities, experience, knowledge and skills of their students and are constantly transformed by them.

Inclusion also implies boundaries around an entity within which and from which exclusion can occur. Many studies of inclusion focus on particular schools. This can cut off an understanding of inclusion within schools from the resources and exclusionary pressures outside them. In focusing on schools, we can miss the way schools themselves contribute to exclusion in the multiplicity of selections between schools, on the basis of class, attainment, faith and disability. It is more fertile to see inclusion in terms of an area within which schools are located. We have focused on a city as our area. This allows questions to be raised, not only about schools and their surrounding communities, but also about what it means to be part of a city, to be a participating citizen.

Inclusion and comprehensive community education

We continue to identify inclusion with the development of comprehensive, community education (Booth and Potts 1983). Such a project is reflected in part, within other European education systems as 'the school for all', although the latter idea loses the sense of education as being wider than schooling. It is linked more widely internationally, in countries of the North and the South, to the movement for Education for All (Booth 2000a). It is a moral and political movement for developing universal education systems based on equality, entitlement, participation and respect for diversity. Inclusion is a process of putting these values into action.

While the idea of comprehensive community education represents a long tradition of ideas about education, unequivocal central support was given only by Labour governments in the periods 1964–71 and 1974–79 (see Simon 1991). By the time local education authorities were beginning to come to grips with the nature of comprehensive curricula and how they should be taught, there were pressures from government to readopt selection within and between schools. The cusp of support for comprehensive schools in the country as a whole is perhaps best captured in the English literature by David Hargreaves' *The Challenge for the Comprehensive School* (Hargreaves 1982) and his review of secondary school provision within the Inner London Education Authority (Hargreaves 1984). Within three years of this latter report, a Conservative government, committed to reducing alternatives to its own influence, had abolished the ILEA. Local education authorities were reduced in strength and lost almost all of their power to co-ordinate educational development. Comprehensive education was left to be carried forward by those weakened local education authorities and schools that remained committed to it.

Schools were strengthened in rhetoric but pressured in practice to comply with far-reaching centralized policies on curricula and school organization and to act in their individual interests rather than a comprehensive analysis of the educational requirements of their wider communities. An increase in the selection of pupils for oversubscribed schools on a variety of grounds, without an overt increase in the number of grammar schools selecting pupils only of high attainment at eleven-plus, was encouraged by both Conservative and Labour administrations after 1979 (see Benn and Chitty 1996, Booth 2000b, Docking 2000, Walford 2000). In this context, inclusion may seem to involve a strategy for education in opposition to prevailing forces. However, education policy continues to contain an uneasy mixture of inclusive/collaborative and selective/competitive strands, which may be retained more in the interests of appealing to a wide range of voters than of establishing a coherent basis for education.

Selection becomes exclusive or excluding when it involves placing differences in value on those rejected or selected. Exclusion is not defined in terms of particular practices, but in terms of the links of such practices to the way people are valued. Compulsory exclusion commonly involves devaluation, although devalued groups may themselves group together in order to counter devaluation, and may compulsorily exclude others in the process. Arguments about selection may take the form of disputes over whether a particular practice – say the placing of children in grammar or special schools – involves devaluation, or over whether it matters if some people are given a lesser value than others. These are some of the further ways in which discussions of inclusion/exclusion need to become more complex.

Comprehensive community education arises out of political movements concerned with the reduction of inequality in access, participation, status and wealth in society. It is about what, in other contexts, gets called, 'equity' or 'social justice' (Gillborn and Youdell 2000), although unfortunately writers who frame their concerns with these other terms rarely make links with the work on inclusion. Thus our definition of inclusion is linked to wider political issues, echoed to an extent within government policies to reduce 'social exclusion'. Once the political and moral underpinnings of inclusion are made explicit, it is clear why it is so contentious. In the UK there appears to be a cultural imperative to argue for inclusion, and given the distance of government policies from the ideals of comprehensive community education and the political ideas that give rise to them, this encourages policy confusion at best and hypocrisy at worst.

INCLUSION IN GOVERNMENT POLICY?

Inclusion and comprehensive community education require a strong *explicit* connection to be made between educational and social policy, a connection which has apparently been lost in government education strategies (see Booth 2000b). The consequences of education policies for the social fabric of cities have been largely ignored, although the racial conflicts of 2001 in northern cities led to a series of reports emphasizing the effects of faith schools in exacerbating ethnic divisions. (See Home Office 2001a and b, and Chapter 5)

The lack of official support for a comprehensive system of education and the encouragement of a whole variety of forms of selection within and between schools distances overall government policy from our definition of inclusion. The competitive school market adds to the burdens on schools working in the most difficult areas and places excluding pressures on many students living in those areas. A government committed to the role of education in building up communities might set itself a target of avoiding the closure of inner city schools, rather than pursuing policies which lead inevitably to the closure of schools within areas under the most stresses (Johnson 1999, Davies 2000). The policies have other effects. They tend to encourage a particular view of school leadership in which quick results for which a head can take responsibility may be valued over long-term, participative sustainable improvements shared and owned by all staff.

At the same time as the increase in competitive pressures, there is an unprecedented interest from the government in 'inclusion', said to be the 'cornerstone' of its policies (DFEE 1998: 8). There is evidence of both narrow and broad views of inclusion within policy. Some aspects of policy focus on identifying and supporting particular groups, while others are linked to the creation of systems that value a diversity of students learning together and might lead to a lessening of the need for categorization. There is a lack of connection between the varieties of inclusion policies. For example, more connection might be made between the Healthy Schools initiative (Denman *et al.* 2002), which encourages a broad review of schools, approaches to school evaluation from OFSTED and the Index for Inclusion (Booth and Ainscow 2002). The efforts to single out particular groups may contribute less to inclusion than exclusion. The requirement that schools identify certain students as 'gifted' or 'talented' or both (DFEE 1999) and then single them out for special attention, creates particular pressures on schools trying to develop inclusion as an approach for all students.

Perhaps the broadest conception of inclusion within government policy-making emanates from the Social Exclusion Unit. This group within the Cabinet Office has examined a range of issues concerned with exclusion in relation to truancy, behaviour, looked-after children (children in public care) and teenage pregnancy as well as a broader examination of ways of over-coming community stresses brought about by poverty and lack of housing and recreational space (see SEU 1998, 2000a, 2000b, 2001).

An inclusive framework for education?

The idea that there would be a solid framework for education on which an inclusive system could be built is currently out of commission. There has been a dismantling of the framework for education which is being replaced in the state sector by semi-autonomous schools supported by an assortment of weakened LEAs, Education Action Zones, private firms, and consultants. These trends have been exacerbated by educational reform by 'eye-catching initiative', in the words of Tony Blair's leaked memo of July 2000. In that memo he expressed concern that the government was being seen as 'soft' on asylum seekers and crime, standing up for Britain and the family. He asked colleagues to come up with 'two or three eye-catching initiatives that are entirely conventional in terms of their attitude to the family' (*Guardian*, 18 July 2000). There is an equal emphasis in the development of education by 'initiatives' which create pools of money for which schools and local education authorities have to bid and use without any guarantee of continuity and hence without building them into their own development structures.

The privatization of education has accelerated. Before the election of May 2001, the future Secretary of State for Education argued for a shift from using the private sector only when local education authorities were failing towards a position of greater legitimacy:

> I'm actually ill at ease, if you want to know the truth, between the fact that where we are at the moment in the private sector is mainly working in LEAs that are struggling and that are failing, and if I'm really serious about saying the private sector has something to offer education, it's got to have something to offer education where it's succeeding as where it's failing. I'm not at ease with our only turning to it when the public sector has failed.
> (Estelle Morris, BBC Radio 4 *You and Yours*, 10 October 2000)

The way in which the balance between public and private providers has shifted was brought home to me in my encounter with the Connexions initiative for provision to support 14–19 year olds in the transition between education, further education and work. The contract for producing the materials to train around 30,000 staff, went to a 'social business' called INCLUDE, formally known as Cities in Schools and specializing in services for students excluded from school for disciplinary reasons. This company was subsequently incorporated into CFBT (Centre for British Teachers). There was no tendering process, but the contract was given on the strength of a small task INCLUDE was carrying out for the Home Office. Institutions of higher education with considerable expertise in the area were given no opportunity to bid for the contract. I discovered this while in direct conversation with those working on the project from INCLUDE/CFBT and the Department for Education and Employment representative. This situation differs markedly from the strict requirement placed on LEAs in allocating contracts.

Inclusion and standards

The raising of 'standards' has formed the main motif for the development of education policy, by a succession of governments; this was encapsulated by the introduction by New Labour of the numeracy and literacy hours. A series of governments has pointed to low expectations for the achievements of students, and the literacy and numeracy hours were to address such apparently persistent failings (Docking 2000). They could be seen as having an inclusive aim, spreading the achievements of the minority of students to the majority. The particular approach to raising standards taken by governments has also been seen to be in conflict with inclusion, encouraging schools to compete for the students most likely to produce good statistics for the school and to avoid taking students who might lower the statistical average or are seen as difficult to teach. OFSTED documents suggest that there is no conflict between the inclusion and the standards agenda. According to OFSTED guidance on inclusion: 'Effective schools are educationally inclusive schools' (OFSTED 2000a: 7) If this is meant to imply that 'an effective' school is defined as one that serves all children in its surrounding communities, then it can be true. If it implies that by serving all children within its surrounding communities, a school will thereby increase average attainments in English and maths as measured by national tests, then it is false, and would certainly involve going against the tide of government policies which set schools to compete for students across catchment boundaries. Every teacher knows that an increase in the numbers of children from middle-class families who have the material and educational capital to support school attainment makes it easier to achieve an increase in the performance of the school on attainment measures.

Gillborn and Youdell (2000) have examined the effects of government policies for raising standards on the disparities in achievement of different groups. They argue that schools and teachers are pushed by these policies to 'ration' education in such a way as to increasingly disadvantage some students. They conclude that such policies have created 'enormous disparities of experience, achievement and esteem between young people' differing in gender, ethnicity and social class:

> The wider education system, policy makers, headteachers, and teachers are currently remarkably busy remaking and reinforcing inequality, especially in relation to 'race' and social class.
>
> (Gillborn and Youdell 2000: 222)

However, many teachers vehemently resist such pressures to increase inequality, and many schools actively incorporate government policies into their own inclusive framework.

A recognition that inclusion provides a moral basis for education can reveal the limitations in elevating the raising of educational standards to a central educational aim. The authors of a report, *Improving City Schools: Strategies to Promote Educational Inclusion*, argued that 'at best, all the energy of the school serves the same end: raising standards' (OFSTED 2000b: 7). This is a parody of inclusion: it implies that inclusion is to be adopted because it contributes to the raising of standards not because it is a virtuous way of engaging together in education (see MacIntyre 1981). There are more important aims of education than the raising of standards; in fact, it is doubtful whether the raising of standards is a legitimate aim of education at all. Raising 'standards' has meaning because the acquisition of knowledge and skills and interests is enriching and pleasurable and gives us power over the development of our lives. It is the means not the end. Education itself is both an end and the means. For me, a fundamental aim of education is to contribute to the development of sustainable ways of life in sustainable environments. Inclusion in the city is as much about the development of cities as it is about the development of education.

Inclusion as a special need

Since 1997, a set of documents on children categorized as having special educational needs, discuss inclusion largely in relation to providing access to the mainstream. The earlier versions of these documents display an equivocal view about whether inclusion implies the reduction of numbers of students in special schools. But persistent lobbying, particularly from organizations of disabled people, has meant that legislation has been passed which has considerably limited the circumstances under which compulsory segregation is permitted (DFES 2001). It is made clear in the inclusion guidance in relation to the Act that schools and local education authorities must strive to make the education of children with 'statements of special educational needs' compatible with the 'efficient' education of others. Although 'minor reasons' had been used to 'block a child's inclusion' in the past, this has to cease:

> Where a child has a statement, mainstream education can only be refused, against parental wishes, where the child's inclusion would be incompatible with the efficient education of other children . . . [this] efficient education caveat must not be abused . . . the Secretary of State will not hesitate to act if she or he believes a maintained school or local education authority was acting unreasonably.
>
> (DFES 2001: 13)

The renewed effort that must be made to avoid the exclusion of students is perhaps clearest in the examples given about children categorized as 'having emotional and behavioural difficulties'. For example, in relation to a secondary age student, the teachers are expected to provide a key worker, use techniques which avoid confrontation, and public shame, be trained in 'de-escalation', put in place the teaching of conflict resolution strategies, and create strong home-school links. This careful advice in statutory guidance contrasts markedly with a series of government speeches blaming parents and threatening to cut any benefits to parents whose children persistently disrupt or play truant (*Guardian*, 29–30 April 2002).

Inclusion as an approach to education

All teachers are required to consider inclusion principles and practices through the detailed statutory guidance provided in the national curriculum which makes inclusion an underlying principle for education rather than a limited set of practices associated with particular children. The guidance for initial teacher education is similarly explicit. Teachers are asked to adopt some of the elements of a pedagogy for diversity by promoting 'active learning' and 'independent learning strategies which enable pupils to think for themselves and to plan and manage their own learning' (p. 93). They are to be prepared so that they 'create a classroom environment which reflects the cultural and linguistic diversity of the class and of society and prepares pupils for living in a diverse and increasingly interdependent society'. The measures they need to take include 'presenting positive images of the achievements of all groups, including, for example, children and adults with disabilities' and 'flexible grouping strategies which give pupils opportunities to experience working cooperatively with peers from diverse backgrounds and with different needs' (Teacher Training Agency 2001: 110–111).

There are barriers to putting such advice into practice. Within teacher education there may be a similar pressure on fulfilling a crowded curriculum, which can lead to didactic teaching styles. The advice conflicts with other aspects of government policy which encourage attainment grouping, and whole-class teaching and an approach to the curriculum in which the absorption of a canon of facts may be given priority over active learning.

Inclusion in school evaluation

There are also detailed evaluation criteria for the development of inclusion in which all OFSTED inspectors are meant to have been trained (OFSTED: 2000a). This document endorses an expansive view of inclusion:

> Educational inclusion is more than a concern about any one group of pupils such as those pupils who have been or are likely to be excluded from school. Its scope is broad. It is about equal opportunities for all pupils, whatever their age, gender, ethnicity, attainment or background.
>
> (OFSTED 2000a: 4)

It is linked particularly to the government endorsement of recommendations from the MacPherson Inquiry into the handling by the police of the murder of a black teenager, Stephen Lawrence. The report adopted the concept of institutional racism:

> The collective failure of an organisation to provide an appropriate and professional service to people because of their colour, culture, or ethnic origin. It can be seen or detected in processes, attitudes and behaviour which amount to discrimination through unwitting prejudice, ignorance, thoughtlessness and racist stereotyping which disadvantage minority ethnic people.
>
> It persists because of the failure of the organisation openly and adequately to recognise and address its existence and causes by policy, example and leadership. Without recognition and action to eliminate such racism it can prevail as part of the ethos or culture of the organisation. It is a corrosive disease.
>
> (MacPherson 1999: 6.34)

An examination of the implications of such ideas may require considerable and deep institutional reform. In order to examine the extent to which the school seeks to counter such institutional racism inspectors are asked to 'judge whether the school promotes respect and understanding of diverse cultures, languages and ethnic groups including faith groups, travellers, asylum seekers and refugees' (OFSTED 2000a: 23). Schools are asked to 'show respect to pupils by using culturally sensitive language, and [to be] alert to the cultural differences in non-verbal communication' (p. 18). They are asked to examine practices in detail, by asking questions such as:

Does the school teach pupils to appreciate their own cultural traditions and the diversities and richness of other cultures?

What action is being taken by the school to promote racial harmony, to prepare pupils for living in a diverse and increasingly interdependent society and specifically to prevent and address racism, sexism and other forms of discrimination?

(OFSTED 2000a: 23, 9)

This last question is significant in linking institutional discrimination in relation to race to other forms of discrimination although the pervasiveness of disablism, class prejudice and homophobia are not mentioned specifically. The extent to which inspectors take on a deep analysis of institutional discrimination since the advent of this new guidance is not clear, although Osler and Morrison's earlier review for the Commission for Racial Equality suggested that they rarely gave such issues a central place in their reports and seemed unaware of their role in such matters (Osler and Morrison 2000).

The Index for Inclusion

The *Index for Inclusion* (Booth and Ainscow 2002) was not produced within a government department, but the first edition was distributed by the DFES to every school in England and therefore clearly had the approval of government. This is confirmed in statutory guidance, which recommends that schools use it to 'identify and remove . . . barriers to learning and participation' and claims that 'schools that have adopted this sort of approach have seen standards rise for all of their pupils' (DFES 2001: 3). The *Index* is a set of materials designed to support the inclusive development of the cultures, policies and practices of schools. It is about making schools reflect and be responsive to all aspects of diversity. It is thus concerned with reducing all forms of personal and institutional discrimination. It is a deliberate attempt to counter the excesses of government policies which have emphasized achievement without putting in place the development of cultures, values and communities which sustain development and give meaning to the variety of student achievements. It is about an approach to school development which is supportive rather than inspectorial, and the authors and publishers have resisted attempts to link it to the award of a Kitemark for inclusion. In the *Index*, an inclusive school is one that is on the move, whatever its initial starting point. It is concerned with all aspects of schools, in staffrooms, classrooms and playgrounds, and in relationships within and between all staff and students and between schools, parents/carers and other members of the surrounding communities. The *Index* sees inclusion as an approach to education integrated into existing arrangements for school development rather than as an extra initiative. It has been used in many schools nationally and has been adopted internationally with translations into several languages.

The *Index* has been influential in helping to create a way of thinking about educational difficulties and ways to overcome them that avoids the language of 'special educational needs'. The notion of special educational needs is replaced by the concept of barriers to learning and participation. Whereas 'special educational needs' directs attention at the deficits of students as the cause of educational difficulties, barriers to learning and participation are seen to arise in all aspects of schools and communities, and at all levels of the system. 'Resources to support learning and participation' can be mobilized at all such levels. In working with the Index, schools may uncover underutilized resources within students, staff, parents/carers and communities: diversity becomes a resource for learning rather than a problem to overcome. These new terms have been adopted within a number of government documents (OFSTED 2000a, DFES 2001).

Whereas the view of raising standards within government policies is focused on outcomes, the emphasis in the *Index* is on creating the right conditions for teaching and learning. In so doing inclusive development is as much concerned with the conditions for staff as it is for students. Such conditions include having the right number of teachers and avoiding excessive teacher mobility. In the south of England in 2002 there are considerable problems of both teacher supply and teacher turnover. The decision by several local authorities to recruit teachers from other countries who themselves can ill afford to lose them, may increase inclusion locally at the expense of more distant exclusion.

CONCLUDING REMARKS

In this chapter I have examined an approach to inclusion and some of the inclusion strands of government policy. The study of inclusion is concerned with all forms of grouping and selection. The issues examined in this book are a sample of those that could have been looked at. For example, the contributors have not looked at the way education systems divide children up according to age. In England there is little stigma associated with moving up a school in an age-cohort; it is almost universal in secondary schools and the predominant arrangement in primary schools. Nevertheless, there are strong values relating age to privilege and maturity. For example, younger age groups may experience devaluation in schools. The potential for grouping by age to be associated with a differing social status is present in all schools and needs to be countered in those attempting to promote inclusion.

The development of inclusion involves shifting the complex balance of including and excluding pressures. Nationally, the emphases on inclusion in government documents provide opportunities to push against the more excluding effects of other policies. Where policies are in opposition, compliance with one may mean non-compliance with another. This can create space to justify choosing those actions which are in accordance with one's values. However, in a city the size of Birmingham, it is extremely difficult to say when inclusion is proceeding. We can look at aspects of inclusion by taking measures of child and adult poverty, or of student school attendance or of teacher supply or of student and staff mobility. Yet capturing changes towards more inclusive cultures will often involve subtle interpretations. The setting out of some of the complexities of inclusion and exclusion, in this chapter and in the book as a whole, provides a real context for making educational decisions and choices.

REFERENCES

Barber, M. (1996) *The Learning Game*, London: Gollancz.

Benn, C. and Chitty, C. (1996) *Thirty Years On: Is Comprehensive Education Alive and Well or Struggling to Survive?* London: Fulton.

Booth, T. (2000a) *Progress in inclusion*, Thematic report summaries, Paris: UNESCO.

Booth, T. (2000b) in Armstrong, F., Armstrong, D., and Barton, L. (2000) 'Inclusion and Exclusion Policy in England: Who Controls the Agenda?' in *Inclusive Education; Policy, Contexts and Comparative Perspectives*, London: Fulton.

Booth, T. and Ainscow, M. (2002) *The Index for Inclusion* (2nd edition), Bristol: Centre for Studies on Inclusive Education.

Booth, T. and Potts, P. (eds) (1983) *Integrating Special Education*, Oxford: Blackwell.

Davies, N. (2000) *The School Report: Why Britain's Schools Are Failing*, London: Vintage.

Denman, S., Moon, A., Parsons, P. and Stears, D. (2002) *The Health Promoting School: Policy Research and Practice*, London: Routledge.

Department for Education and Employment (DFEE) (1998) *Meeting Special Educational Needs: A Programme of Action*, London: DFEE.

Department for Education and Employment (DFEE) (1999) *Excellence in Cities*, London: Stationery Office.

Department for Education and Science (DES) (1986) Education Act, London: HMSO.

Department for Education and Skills (DFES) (2001) *Inclusive Schooling: Children with Special Educational Needs*, London: DFES.

Dixon, A., Drummond, M.J., Hart, S. and McIntyre, D. (2002) *Learning Without Limits*, Milton Keynes: Open University Press.

Docking, J. (ed.) (2000) *New Labour's Policies for Schools: Raising the Standard?* London: Fulton.

Fielding, M. (1999) 'Communities of learners', in O'Hagan, R. (ed.) *Modern Educational Myths*, London: Kogan Page.

Gillborn, D. and Youdell, D. (2000) *Rationing Education: Policy, Practice, Reform and Equity*, Buckingham: Open University Press.

Hargreaves, D. (1982) *The Challenge for the Comprehensive School; Culture, Curriculum and Community*, London: Routledge & Kegan Paul.

Hargreaves, D. (1984) *Improving Secondary Schools*, London: Inner London Education Authority.

Home Office (2001a) *Building Cohesive Communities, A Report of the Ministerial Group on Public Order and Community Cohesion*, London: the Stationery Office.

Home Office (2001b) *Community Cohesion, A Report of the Independent Review Team*, chaired by Ted Cantle, London: Home Office.

Johnson, M. (1999) *Failing School, Failing City*, Charlbury: Jon Carpenter.

MacIntyre, A. (1981) *After Virtue*, London: Duckworth.

MacPherson, W. (1999) *The Stephen Lawrence Inquiry*, London: HMSO.

Office for Standards in Education (OFSTED) (2000a) *Evaluating Educational Inclusion*, London: OFSTED.

Office for Standards in Education (OFSTED) (2000b) *Improving City Schools; Strategies to Promote Educational Inclusion*, London: OFSTED.

Osler, A. and Morrison, M. (2000) *Inspecting Schools for Race Equality; OFSTED's Strengths and Weaknesses*, London: Trentham Books/Commission for Racial Equality.

Simon, B. (1991) *Education and the Social Order 1940–1990*, London: Lawrence and Wishart.

Social Exclusion Unit (1998) *Bringing Britain Together: A National Strategy for Neighbourhood Renewal*, London: the Stationery Office.

Social Exclusion Unit (2000a) *Minority Ethnic Issues in Social Exclusion and Neighbourhood Renewal*, London: Cabinet Office.

Social Exclusion Unit (2000b) *National Strategy for Neighbourhood Renewal: Policy Action Team Report Summaries: A Compendium*, London: the Stationery Office.

Social Exclusion Unit (2001) *Preventing Social Exclusion*, London: the Stationery Office.

Teacher Training Agency (2001) *Handbook to Accompany the Standards for the Award of Qualified Teacher Status and Requirements for the Provision of Initial Teacher Training*, London: TTA.

Walford, G. (2000) *Policy and Politics in Education*, Aldershot: Ashgate.

Williams, R. (1976) *Keywords*, London: Fontana.

SUTTON FOUR OAKS

SUTTON VESEY

SUTTON NEW HALL

OSCOTT

KINGSTANDING

PERRY BARR

ERDINGTON

SANDWELL

STOCKLAND GREEN

KINGSBURY

HANDSWORTH

ASTON

SOHO

WASHWOOD HEATH

HODGE HILL

LADYWOOD

NECHELLS

SHARD END

SMALL HEATH

YARDLEY

SPARKBROOK

QUINTON

EDGBASTON

ACOCKS GREEN

SHELDON

HARBORNE

SPARKHILL

FOX HOLLIES

BARTLEY GREEN

SELLY OAK

MOSELEY

WEOLEY

HALL GREEN

BOURNVILLE

LONGBRIDGE

NORTHFIELD

KING'S NORTON

BRANDWOOD

BILLESLEY

Birmingham's political wards

Chapter 2

'A great learning city'

Patricia Potts

INTRODUCTION

Chapter 1 provides a UK national perspective on inclusion/exclusion and discusses the approach of our research team. In this chapter I am going to look at the city of Birmingham's approach to inclusive education, focusing on the years between 1993 and 2001. I discuss attempts to develop an agreed policy for moving towards greater inclusion and set them in the context of the Education Department's overall priorities. Chapter 3 illustrates the views of policy-makers and practitioners on these developments. There is no single or accurate account that can be given of attempts to develop policies for inclusion in education in the city, and you will see that there are inconsistencies and disagreements within and between the views of our participants. The history, scale and complexity of the city's education services and the consequent difficulty of developing and implementing coherent policies for change form the context for the detailed case studies that follow in Chapters 4–8.

Birmingham is a multicultural city with substantial Pakistani, Chinese and Afro-Caribbean communities, many of whose members are third-generation British. However, ethnic homogeneity rather than diversity characterizes some areas of the city. Many Asians live in inner-city or inner suburban areas and work in family businesses, while in the outer city there are white working-class areas of high unemployment.

There are also gender divisions. For example, the outer-city manufacturing industries, providing jobs mainly for men, have either disappeared or are under threat. Service industries, in city centre hotels and outer-city shopping malls, are expanding, providing mostly part-time and seasonal jobs with unsocial working hours, most of which are undertaken by women. Gender demarcation, in jobs, attitudes and expectations, emerged as a theme of our observations and conversations across the city (see Chapter 6).

Features of a cityscape

Standing on the brow of a hill in the English Midlands, the civic centre of Birmingham was once surrounded by the commercial enterprises that made its fortune, especially those involving metalwork: jewellery, weapons and, later, cars. Birmingham was known as the 'city of a thousand trades'. Close by the inner industrial ring were dense terraces of workers' houses leading out to leafier suburbs and villages, some of them still identifiable within the urban sprawl.

During the second half of the nineteenth century, Birmingham grew rapidly as a centre of manufacturing and political influence. Liberals – notably the Chamberlain family – ran the city and, although there has been a safe Labour majority in the elected Council since 1984, there is regular cross-party cooperation. Examples include the decisions to build the international conference centre and to focus on developing Birmingham's service industries.

During the twentieth century, Birmingham experienced several periods of major reconstruction, beginning with inner-city slum clearance in the 1930s. Whole communities were moved out to new estates on the edge of the city, where the land was cheaper and agricultural activity in decline anyway. Green and spacious suburban council housing replaced the dark and insanitary terraces where everyone had lived on the street. For health reasons, houses and factories were segregated into different zones, which meant people had to travel between them and they were connected by new roads and public transport. Although one resident said their new house was 'Shangri-la to our Ma', even then others said 'the layout of the estates made them soulless and monotonous' (quotations from the 'Visions of Birmingham' exhibition, Birmingham Museum and Art Gallery 1999–2000).

Thirty years later, the city was transformed by the decline in the older industries and the rise in the manufacture and use of the car. New factories were built on the outskirts of town – Longbridge, for example – and the city was veined with new roads. The inner ring road (which had first been proposed in 1917) came to be known as the 'concrete collar', and 'Spaghetti Junction', linking the city to the new M1 motorway, became an image of modern Birmingham. The redeveloped Bull Ring was opened in 1964 as 'the ultimate shopping experience'.

From the 1980s, the civic centre underwent a transformation, reinventing itself as a commercial and cultural venue, symbolized by the redevelopment of the jewellery and mill quarter, the National Indoor Arena (1991) and the creative heights to which Simon Rattle took the City of Birmingham Symphony Orchestra in the concert hall of the International Convention Centre (also opened in 1991). In the 1960s, pedestrians were placed below the automobile, roads above underpasses. Now this was reversed. The city centre was pedestrianized and the traffic put out of sight underground. To

Figure 2 Birmingham city centre in 1905 © Crown Copyright.

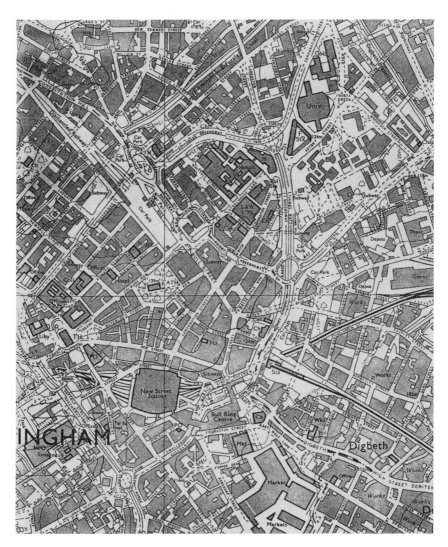

Figure 3 Birmingham city centre in 1983 © Crown Copyright.

Figure 4 Birmingham's 'Spaghetti Junction' on the MI: a national symbol of post-war modernization

the south-east of the city the National Exhibition Centre (1976) and the expanding International Airport (1984) complement the resurgence of the centre, where the programme of regeneration still continues with the redevelopment of the area around the Bull Ring.

An IKON of regeneration

A mixture of restoration and redevelopment characterizes the area around the canal in the city centre. The IKON Gallery, a restored and converted late-nineteenth-century school, shines at the heart of the new Brindleyplace. 'Dropped from a great height' into a space between the factories, Oozells Street School, one of the first post-Forster Education Act schools, opened in 1878 with 807 children; it cost the pupils' families a penny a week. Only twenty years later, the 'rapid destruction of small house property' nearby, together with 'burgling and flooding', led to the recommendation that the

Figure 5 From school to gallery: an icon of Birmingham's regeneration, the IKON Gallery
© Gary Kirkham

Figure 6 Anthony Gormley's 'The Iron Man' in the city of a thousand metal trades

school be closed. In 1898, the building was reopened as George Dixon Higher Grade School, teaching science and technology to secondary-aged students. This was one of just three secondary schools in the city and it was neither compulsory nor free. In 1906, George Dixon moved out and the building became a pupil teachers' centre for girls and young women aged fifteen and over. In effect, the school was a girls' grammar school, but it also functioned as a city technical college specializing in the skills required for local metal industries. From 1929, the college provided lunchtime courses for workers in maths, English, history and languages. In 1981, the building was awarded a Grade II listing, which saved it from the redevelopment that was beginning in the area and at the same time the IKON Gallery (1963) was looking for a new home. The converted school is a shell, with a polychrome exterior and a white interior. Once a dominating presence wedged between Victorian commercial buildings, the school now glows in its own separate space beside the chunky buildings of the new square (see Upton 1998). Though George Dixon School still exists, as a secondary school with a sixth-form centre, Oozells Street School is no longer a community of children.

Regeneration and education

The relationship between learners and city regeneration is a central issue for this book. National and local initiatives in education are, today, often aimed at the renewal of urban communities, both economically and socially. For example, the 1999 government report *Excellence in Cities* (DFEE 1999) stated: 'Above all, inner cities are often characterised by expectations of pupils that are too low, by parental and pupil anxiety, by a culture of under-achievement and by a perception that failure is endemic.'

Education is also a core issue in the government's 'New Commitment to Neighbourhood Renewal', an interdisciplinary strategy to encourage the running of local communities by local residents. Problems the strategy aims to tackle include: 'worklessness, crime, low skills, poor health, housing and the physical environment' (Social Exclusion Unit 2001: 57). Birmingham is one of the fifty local authorities whose level of deprivation makes it eligible for the Neighbourhood Renewal Fund. The report ends with a list of 105 specific 'key commitments', for example:

> Promotion of social inclusion to be a key element in Local Transport Plans . . . Extension of Excellence in Cities to cover 2,000 schools. . . . Special help for the most seriously under-achieving schools. . . . At least £600 million to tackle truancy and school exclusion. . . . Development of neighbourhood learning centres. . . . £252 million to establish 6,000 UK online centres by 2002. Every deprived area to have at least one accessible, community-based facility.
>
> (op. cit.: 61–67)

Welcoming this report, Secretary of State for Education Estelle Morris said:

> In some of Britain's most deprived areas schools are one of the few solid centres of community life. And they are one of the few stable factors in the lives of some of Britain's most disadvantaged children. Only by ensuring that everyone receives a high quality education can we have opportunity for all, social justice and rising prosperity. A good education is the best route out of deprivation.
>
> (Press notice, 16 November 2001)

In Birmingham, as in other cities, inner-city redevelopment does not routinely include families and schools. Unlike the schemes for neighbourhood renewal, which focus on inter-agency support for residential areas, particularly public housing estates, inner-city renewal focuses on commerce and the construction of housing largely for young or childless workers. In his book *The Chosen City*, Nicholas Schoon points out that 'In large areas of our conurbations almost all of the resident children belong to the poor' (Schoon 2001: 175). They are not likely to be provided for within schemes for inner-city renewal, but Schoon argues that schools should be at the heart of all regeneration plans because:

> It is bad news for the city if parents with jobs and aspirations feel they need to move out because they cannot trust the local schools. . . . An urban renaissance that is based on luring prosperous but invariably childless households into the city isn't worthy of the name; it has to bring in toddlers and teenagers too. . . . The fact that schools tend to drive people with choices out of large towns and cities is particularly tragic because these should be the best place to combine satisfying work with raising a family.
>
> (ibid.: 175, 181)

This means that housing and schooling have to be planned for together, but, given that most neighbourhoods are not socially mixed:

> Delivering real equality of opportunity in education would require either much more redistribution of resources to the schools in poor areas or an evening out of the intakes, ensuring every school had roughly the same mix of social classes and abilities. . . . Such schools could be a very effective way of attacking counter-urbanisation.
>
> (ibid.: 183, 185)

Schoon argues that selection by ability and owner-occupier housing are necessary to the creation of popular city schools. However, he acknowledges that many parents reject city state schools for reasons other than that of poor exam results. If a school could show that its students were better taught, more stimulated and less underachieving than a suburban school where the students were coasting along, this still wouldn't attract those 'who are as concerned about the social class or race of their children's classmates as about the quality of teaching' (op. cit.: 186). The desire for homogeneity shown by this kind of family is echoed, in different versions, in strategies for urban renewal based on the idea of a fixed geographical zone, which, though aimed at raising educational attainment, do not address wider issues of social inclusion and exclusion (see below and Chapter 8).

In Birmingham, despite the success of many social housing, as well as economic and cultural, schemes regeneration has not affected the whole city. Figures for unemployment, poor child health, one-parent families and homelessness are higher than national averages, much higher in some areas. The chair of the Council's Education Committee described the city as having 'pockets of affluence'. Areas once described as 'luxury beyond our wildest dreams' have become isolated and depressed, cut off by poverty and distance from the revitalized city centre.

Education in Birmingham

The population of Birmingham, the UK's 'second city', is around one million (London has around eight million) and, following the abolition of the Inner London and Strathclyde authorities in the late 1980s, Birmingham City Council became the largest education authority in the UK. This is now disputed by the county of Kent, whose website says that it contains over 600 schools, with more than 200,000 students, serving a population of 1.3 million.

Educational provision in Birmingham is labyrinthine. There is widespread selection by attainment, gender, wealth and religion into hierarchies of independent, foundation, voluntary-aided and state (or 'community') mainstream and special schools. There are also three sixth-form colleges and fifteen providers of further education registered with the local Learning and Skills Council (though this number underestimates the total range of provision): '[There are] about 450 institutions and almost every type of school you can think of has at least one representative in Birmingham, which is confusing to say the least' (chair, Council Education Committee).

About 10 per cent of the 180,000 school students attend selective grammar schools (state and independent). Specialized provision for disabled students, students of assumed low ability and students who experience social difficulties is also extensive: there are just under thirty special schools and thirty-eight special units attached to mainstream primary and secondary schools. In 1998, the proportion of students with statements of special educational needs in segregated as opposed to mainstream settings in Birmingham was 62 per cent, compared with a national average of just over 36 per cent.

Single-sex education is a high priority, especially for Asian parents of girls, and one school has grown into the largest secondary school for girls in Europe, with more than 1,600 students (see Chapter 6):

> In the city as a whole we have got about twice as many places available for girls as for boys in single-sex education but the girls' schools are all in the wrong places. If we could move [them] it would solve a lot of the issues.
>
> (chair, Education Committee)

The daily criss-crossing of the city by students attending schools outside their home communities is a major characteristic of education in Birmingham (see Chapter 8).

Educational reform in Birmingham 1993–2001

At the time of our research, Birmingham's Education Department had just been reorganized into seven divisions (see diagrams on pages 27–29 for pre–1993 and post-1993 structures). Under the revised structure, the chief education officer was responsible for management and coordination, direct services and the advisory and support service, while his deputy oversaw special educational needs (SEN), finance, personnel and equalities and early years and school support. The functions of several of the divisions appeared to be closely related, if not actually overlapping and the issue of cross-divisional collaboration emerged as a theme from our conversations with education officers, administrators and practitioners.

For example, the Advisory and Support Service (BASS) is not only structurally separate from the special educational needs (SEN) division but is also geographically distant. Further, as a result of the history of the Education Department, the advisors for special educational needs are in the advisory and support service division not the special educational needs division. Each of these two divisions has developed its own ethos and contact between them remains limited. While the SEN division has been generously funded to carry out its statutory responsibilities, BASS has had to become more entrepreneurial and now provides training for schools as a trading company. Colleagues have expressed the view that this makes the division more accountable.

In 1993, a high-profile critic of the then Conservative government was appointed as Birmingham's chief education officer (CEO). His arrival marked the beginning of a period of enormous activity in the city's Education Department and the drafting of a policy for inclusive education took place in the context of renewed debate about principles and priorities. For example, the chair of the elected Council's education committee published a document in 1994 entitled *A Great Learning City*, in which he stated that:

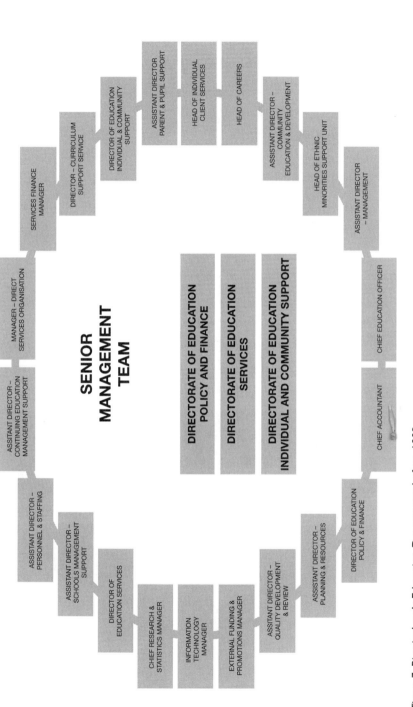

SENIOR MANAGEMENT TEAM

DIRECTORATE OF EDUCATION POLICY AND FINANCE

DIRECTORATE OF EDUCATION SERVICES

DIRECTORATE OF EDUCATION INDIVIDUAL AND COMMUNITY SUPPORT

SERVICES FINANCE MANAGER

DIRECTOR – CURRICULUM SUPPORT SERVICE

DIRECTOR OF EDUCATION INDIVIDUAL & COMMUNITY SUPPORT

ASSISTANT DIRECTOR – PARENT & PUPIL SUPPORT

HEAD OF INDIVIDUAL CLIENT SERVICES

HEAD OF CAREERS

ASSISTANT DIRECTOR – COMMUNITY EDUCATION & DEVELOPMENT

HEAD OF ETHNIC MINORITIES SUPPORT UNIT

ASSISTANT DIRECTOR – MANAGEMENT

MANAGER – DIRECT SERVICES ORGANISATION

ASSISTANT DIRECTOR – CONTINUING EDUCATION MANAGEMENT SUPPORT

ASSISTANT DIRECTOR – PERSONNEL & STAFFING

ASSISTANT DIRECTOR – SCHOOLS MANAGEMENT SUPPORT

DIRECTOR OF EDUCATION SERVICES

CHIEF RESEARCH & STATISTICS MANAGER

INFORMATION TECHNOLOGY MANAGER

EXTERNAL FUNDING & PROMOTIONS MANAGER

ASSITANT DIRECTOR – QUALITY DEVELOPMENT & REVIEW

ASSISTANT DIRECTOR – PLANNING & RESOURCES

DIRECTOR OF EDUCATION POLICY & FINANCE

CHIEF ACCOUNTANT

CHIEF EDUCATION OFFICER

Figure 7 Birmingham's Education Department before 1993

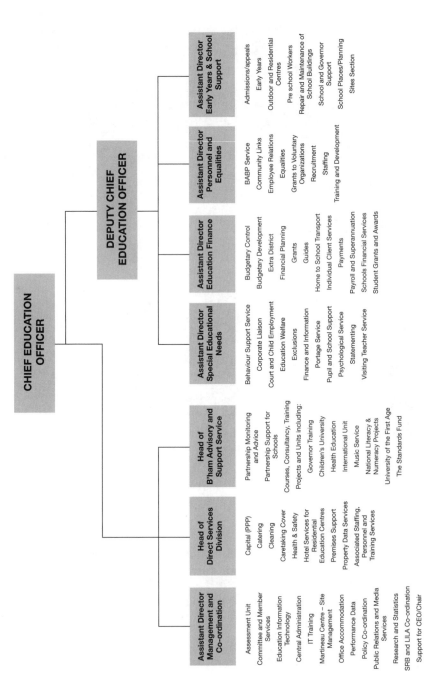

CHIEF EDUCATION OFFICER

DEPUTY CHIEF EDUCATION OFFICER

Assistant Director Management and Co-ordination

Assessment Unit
Committee and Member Services
Education Information Technology
Central Administration
IT Training
Martineau Centre – Site Management
Office Accommodation
Performance Data
Policy Co-ordination
Public Relations and Media Services
Research and Statistics
SRB and LILA Co-ordination
Support for CEO/Chair

Head of Direct Services Division

Capital (PPP)
Catering
Cleaning
Caretaking Cover
Health & Safety
Hotel Services for Residential Education Centres
Premises Support
Property Data Services
Associated Staffing, Personnel and Training Services

Head of B'ham Advisory and Support Service

Partnership Monitoring and Advice
Partnership Support for Schools
Courses, Consultancy, Training
Projects and Units including:
Governor Training
Children's University
Health Education
International Unit
Music Service
National Literacy & Numeracy Projects
University of the First Age
The Standards Fund

Assistant Director Special Educational Needs

Behaviour Support Service
Corporate Liaison
Court and Child Employment
Education Welfare
Exclusions
Finance and Information
Portage Service
Pupil and School Support
Psychological Service
Statementing
Visiting Teacher Service

Assistant Director Education Finance

Budgetary Control
Budgetary Development
Extra District
Financial Planning
Grants
Guides
Home to School Transport
Individual Client Services
Payments
Payroll and Superannuation
Schools Financial Services
Student Grants and Awards

Assistant Director Personnel and Equalities

BABP Service
Community Links
Employee Relations
Equalities
Grants to Voluntary Organizations
Recruitment
Staffing
Training and Development

Assistant Director Early Years & School Support

Admissions/appeals
Early Years
Outdoor and Residential Centres
Pre school Workers
Repair and Maintenance of School Buildings
School and Governor Support
School Places/Planning
Sites Section

Figure 8 The Education Department after 1993

EDUCATION SERVICE STRUCTURE – AUGUST 2000

CHIEF EDUCATION OFFICER
DEPUTY CHIEF EDUCATION OFFICER

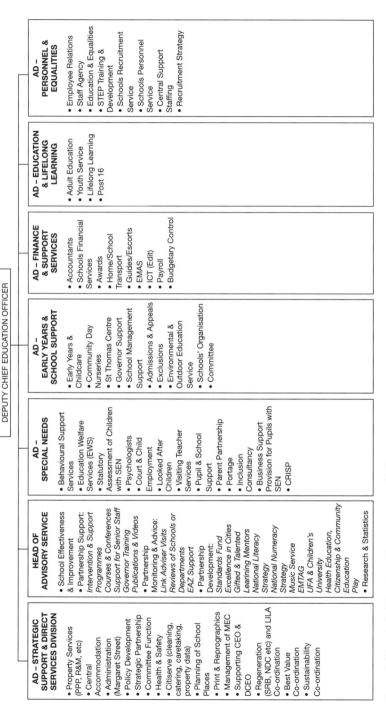

AD – STRATEGIC SUPPORT & DIRECT SERVICES DIVISION

- Property Services (PPP, R&M, etc)
- Central Accommodation (Margaret Street)
- Administration
- Policy Development
- Strategic Partnership
- Committee Function
- Health & Safety
- Citiserve (cleaning, catering, caretaking, property data)
- Planning of School Places
- Print & Reprographics
- Management of MEC
- Supporting CEO & DCEO
- Regeneration (SRB, NDC etc) and LILA Co-ordination
- Best Value Co-ordination
- Sustainability Co-ordination

HEAD OF ADVISORY SERVICE

- School Effectiveness & Improvement
- Partnership Support: *Intervention & Support Programmes*
- *Courses & Conferences Support for Senior Staff*
- *Governor Training*
- *Publications & Videos*
- *Partnership Monitoring & Advice:*
- *Link Adviser Visits*
- *Reviews of Schools or Departments*
- *EAZ Support*
- *Partnership Development:*
- *Standards Fund*
- *Excellence in Cities*
- *Gifted & Talented*
- *Learning Mentors*
- *National Literacy Strategy*
- *National Numeracy Strategy*
- *Music Service*
- *EMTAG*
- *UFA & Children's University*
- *Health Education, Citizenship & Community Education*
- *Play*
- Research & Statistics

AD – SPECIAL NEEDS

- Behavioural Support Services
- Education Welfare Services (EWS)
- Statutory Assessment of Children with SEN
- Psychologists
- Court & Child Employment
- Looked After Children
- Visiting Teacher Services
- Pupil & School Support
- Parent Partnership
- Portage
- Inclusion Consultancy
- Business Support
- Provision for Pupils with SEN
- CRISP

AD – EARLY YEARS & SCHOOL SUPPORT

- Early Years & Childcare
- Community Day Nurseries
- St Thomas Centre
- Governor Support
- School Management Support
- Admissions & Appeals
- Exclusions
- Environmental & Outdoor Education Service
- Schools' Organisation Committee

AD – FINANCE & SUPPORT SERVICES

- Accountants
- Schools Financial Services
- Awards
- Home/School Transport
- Guides/Escorts
- EMAS
- ICT (Edit)
- Payroll
- Budgetary Control

AD – EDUCATION & LIFELONG LEARNING

- Adult Education
- Youth Service
- Lifelong Learning
- Post 16

AD – PERSONNEL & EQUALITIES

- Employee Relations
- Staff Agency
- Education & Equalities
- STEP Training & Development
- Schools Recruitment Service
- Schools Personnel Service
- Central Support Staffing
- Recruitment Strategy

Figure 9 The city's Education Department in 2001

The objective of your [Education] Committee is to present the people of Birmingham with an education service which allows them equality of access and progression to the highest levels of aspiration and achievement and seeks to include all and exclude none.

To start the process of review within his own department, the CEO appointed an education commission, whose report, *Aiming High*, was published in October (Birmingham Education Commission 1993). The report noted that education had not been seen as a high priority in the culture of the City Council and that coordination and communication were often unsatisfactory. The LEA is described as the 'guarantor of standards and rights' but parent witnesses listed several ways in which their children were excluded from education: low expectations, poor transport, under-representation on school governing bodies and ignorance of religious and cultural requirements (para.44, p.12). About 31 per cent of school exclusions and 27 per cent of children in care were black, when the black population of the city was only 9 per cent. Head teacher witnesses described the LEA's 'special needs policy as reactive, without proper preventive work being carried out' (para. 76, p. 21). Special-school head teachers 'felt isolated and let down by the management structure'. However:

> There was also a strong feeling that all children should be entitled to be on the books of a mainstream school in Birmingham, even if they were rarely able to attend it. There should be a policy of inclusion, not exclusion, with every child starting off with the right to a place in a mainstream school.
>
> (para.77, p.21)

Two years later, the commission carried out an evaluation of progress towards the recommendations made in 1993, and *Hitting the Target?* was published in October 1995. A number of developments were noted, including a more positive culture in the Council and the Education Department. However, not all areas of work were proceeding with as much energy. The city had set up an exclusions working party after the first report but the second urges more action 'so that momentum is not lost' (para.18, pp.7/8). An exclusions unit was set up in 1995 (see Chapter 3). In connection with 'special educational needs', the report notes:

> Many of our witnesses felt that special needs had been neglected by the LEA. . . . Another [special school head] referred to Birmingham as a 'Sleeping Giant' where provision for special needs was concerned. It was felt that the expertise in special schools was not being fully utilised.
>
> (para.33, p.13)

A new special educational needs division was created within the Education Department in response to these findings (see diagram on page 28).

The University of the First Age

The University of the First Age (UFA) was an early initiative and one of particular importance to the CEO. An 'innovative concept in urban schooling', it was designed to 'address issues of substantial disaffection and underachievement in early adolescence' and 'increase levels of self esteem and motivation in young people' (Birmingham Education Department leaflet). Secondary-aged students from across the city, especially during Key Stage 3 of the national curriculum, come together for a wide range of activities out of school, within partnership arrangements between clusters of schools, museums, libraries, community centres, arts centres and local supplementary schools.

The first pilot projects took place in 1995, and between 1996 and 2001 the UFA involved 14,000 young people. The original funding came from damages paid to the CEO by ex-Secretary of State for Education John Patten (Conservative) in recompense for slandering him as a 'nutter'. It is now funded from several sources: the Social Regeneration Fund, the Neighbourhood Renewal Fund (both national sources) and an LEA grant (see website: www.ufa.org.uk/pages/about.htm). The CEO makes the link between the UFA and processes of inclusion:

> 'Putting in the notion of changing the nature of schooling at the beginning of secondary level . . . so kids belong to a school and the University of the First Age. . . . Now I think that is a slow-burning bomb under the system. I really deeply do . . . It uses all of Gardner's intelligences. It appeals to emotional intelligence. It brings kids out from single-sex schools. They learn together for a week or a fortnight. And people are going back and saying that this is the best thing that has ever happened to their kids. . . . You get different timetables. You get into preferred learning styles, the whole thing. . . . I passionately believe that the University of the First Age is a mechanism for inclusion.'

The University of the First Age is now a national project.

The funding and re/allocation of resources

A major context for educational reform in the city is, of course, funding. In the early 1990s, Local Management of Schools gave individual schools control over their budgets and left LEAs with a much smaller number of statutory commitments. Schools could buy back from the LEA services that would have been delivered and paid for centrally under the old system. The increased independence of schools, in a culture where they already enjoyed considerable autonomy, made the development of coherent, city-wide, policies for reform as difficult as it was necessary. Schemes aimed at the flexible use of resources to support change drew on funding available, not only within the local authority but also from new government and private sources. Additional funding has gone into projects run from segregated as well as from mainstream schools.

The idea behind the Supported Places Initiative (SPI) of 1994–5 was to provide flexible learning support in the mainstream rather than tie resources (staff hours, equipment and administrative support) to specific students with statements of special educational needs. Nine primary and four secondary schools were involved in a pilot scheme (see Chapter 3 for an appreciative view of this scheme given by a primary school head teacher). A progress report was positive about the learning experiences of the pupils but listed a range of concerns, mostly about budgeting and the small number of children able to receive this additional support. SPI was superseded in 1995 by the Criteria for Special Provision (CRISP), devised by an educational psychologist and based on Coventry's 'Dimensions for Special Provision'. The criteria were designed as a way to establish the extent of need (and therefore need for resources) in schools, but the scheme has been criticized for being resource-rather than student-led.

Around the same time six 'inclusion projects', led by special schools, received LEA funding. Their mission statement contained the following commitment: 'To take a lead in the process of promoting inclusive education, by developing a framework which supports high quality integrative practices.' In 2000, after receiving bids, the LEA allocated Standards Fund money to one mainstream and five special schools to develop 'inclusion networks', whose 'key purposes' were: transferring students from special to mainstream provision, supporting students in mainstream schools and providing inclusive experiences for students remaining in segregated provision. An evaluation report concluded that: 'All the project work contributed to the long-term objective of increasing the capacity of mainstream schools and colleges to educate pupils with special educational needs' (Beech and Chinner 2001: 2).

A third example is the plan for the rebuilding of ten of the city's schools. The Public Private Partnership (PPP) system introduced in 1997, made it possible to embark on work involving capital investment without adding to the city's public sector borrowing requirement. Four of the ten schools identified are close to the area discussed in Chapter 8 (see also the co-location plan between a special and a mainstream school referred to in Chapters 4 and 6). However, the operation of this system is complex and progress is therefore slow. Further, there are about forty-eight schools whose premises are in serious need of repair.

School improvement and the Birmingham Advisory and Support Service (BASS)

A range of initiatives related to the city's priority of school improvement were developed from this division of the Education Department. For example, on the principle that when a butterfly flaps a wing here a hurricane occurs over there, BASS produced the *School Improvement Butterflies Handbook* listing a collection of local curriculum development projects and functioning as a way for local schools to share and exchange ideas and practices. The 'Butterflies' still exist, now run by a multimedia trading company.

'New Outlooks' was another project, looking at a framework for 'behaviour management' in schools, with a working group led by an educational psychologist. This led to the publication of *A Framework for Intervention* trial scheme for the year 1996–7. This is 'really up and running now' says a colleague. She says the project looks at the students' environment. It does not explicitly aim to change staff attitudes but rather to discuss with them how to change the students' 'environment'. 'It works,' she says.

Third, the Families of Schools is an ongoing informal network of school clusters, on which members of staff from the Advisory and Support Services Division (BASS) base their training work. Instead of devising courses for all-comers, BASS designs packages for specific clusters of schools on a commercial basis, depending on their priorities.

Success for All and a Standard for Inclusive Education

Birmingham's Strategy 2000 was part of the city's overall education development plan for 1997. It promoted the concept of 'improving on previous best' as the way to raise standards, and there was more about providing support in the mainstream than on developing specialized services. Around the same time, the city's first advisors for special educational needs were appointed. As with other advisors, they were based in the Advisory and Support Services Division rather than the SEN division, but they had a dual role. One of them was appointed leader of the inclusion team; the other was responsible for developing Birmingham's 'Standard for Inclusive Education'. The aim was for this framework to be used by all schools by 2001.

As part of the city's school improvement strategy, these 'Standards' were developed in a number of areas, including information technology, the creative arts and equal opportunities, as well as inclusive education. Materials were developed for the tasks of auditing, target-setting, action-planning and implementation. Each set of 'Standards' was presented in the same format and organized into sections based on 'seven processes of school improvement' under the topic headings of: leadership, management and organization, learning environment, teaching and learning, staff development, collective review and parental and community involvement. Each 'Standard' is organized under the three headings of 'emergent', 'established' and 'advanced', and, together, the processes and stages form a matrix of twenty-one sections. Each section contains statements describing the position of a hypothetical school. For example, in the 'Standard for Inclusive Education', the first of eight sets of statements under the heading 'Management and Organization' are:

Emergent: Awareness of SEN budget issues;

Established: Key staff, including SENCOs, have a basic understanding of how SEN budget is calculated;

Advanced: Planning process and budget decision on SEN involve governing body, senior management team, SENCO. There is a clear understanding of SEN budget and how it is calculated.

Schools were expected to consider which of the three stages they had reached for each set of statements and to give appropriate evidence on a school audit form. From evidence of 'emergent' or 'established' levels, schools then identified future targets, which form the basis for their action plan under the headings 'action', 'timescale', 'responsibility', 'resources' and 'criteria for success'. The intention was to help schools reflect on their practice, identify strengths and weaknesses and take agreed action to move towards the goal of reaching the 'advanced' level for all statements relating to all seven processes. 'It's good because it allows you to think, or to get away from the idea that an inclusive school is one which is accessible to disabled pupils, it looks into curriculum and teaching and learning styles and management issues' (advisor for SEN and co-author of the 'Standard').

However, it is not clear from the materials themselves whether they were aimed at increasing the participation of 'special' students in mainstream education or at increasing the participation of all students. Some statements focus on specific individuals or groups 'with SEN', implying a deficit model of barriers to learning, whereas others seem to be aimed at changing policies and practices that will affect the whole school, thus implying a more social model (see Figure 10).

We asked the advisor how he saw these different approaches operating within the 'Standard for Inclusive Education':

'What we don't have is a definition which says an inclusive school will look like this because they'll all look slightly different. It doesn't mean that I don't have a view of what inclusion is, because I do. And I try to promote that in everything I do. But this is through the school improvement framework so it's actually looking at how schools can improve what they do and become more inclusive . . . I don't see

Success for Everyone A Standard for Inclusive Educational Practice in Schools

	Emergent	Established	Advanced
Management and Organization	Awareness of SEN budget issues Policies in place, including SEN, Equal Opps, Behaviour, Exclusions which meet basic legal requirements, and including requirements of Disability Discrimination Act School prospectus includes ref. to SEN and SENCO GB has nominated a governor SENCO designated and time allocated with clear responsibilities and job description	Key staff, including SENCO have a basic understanding of how SEN budget is calculated Policies are further developed and review is established practice H/T & SENCO reports regularly to GB Governors have regular meetings with SENCO Implications of the Disability Discrimination Act have been considered School sets targets for inclusion	Planning process and budget decisions on SEN involve GB, SMT, SENCO. There is a clear understanding of SEN budget and how it is calculated Policies are fully integrated in curriculum, have clear success criteria & are reviewed annually or biannually H/T and SENCO report regularly to GB on progress and implementation of policies Governors are fully aware of and trained in inclusion issues and involved in monitoring which informs strategic planning SENCO takes lead in monitoring and evaluating SEN provision with other staff Disability Discrimination Act is embedded in school objectives
Teaching and Learning	School demonstrates commitment to SEN/Equal opportunities in curriculum documents and schemes of work Procedures are in place to ensure early identification and assessment of SEN There are some examples of curriculum approaches which meet a range of individual needs The need for additional learning resources is identified	All curriculum materials and schemes of work provide some guidance about differentiation School is reviewing curriculum materials/learning resources to ensure positive images of SEN/learning disability All curriculum plans address SEN and implementation is monitored All staff implement procedures for the Code of Practice Some teachers are developing a variety of teaching and learning approaches to meet a wide range of individual needs Additional learning resources are targeted at key areas	All schemes of work fully incorporate consideration of a range of learning needs All curriculum materials/learning resources are selected or developed to reflect positive images of disability All staff implement and are involved in a systematic review of CoP procedures All teachers ensure that every individual need is catered for in terms of knowledge, understanding and skills School is deploying appropriate and sufficient resources including staffing to meet a wide range of SEN

Figure 10 Birmingham's Standards for Inclusive Education

	Emergent	Established	Advanced
Leadership	H/T has begun to discuss ways in which school can cater for a wider range of individual needs Senior managers are carrying this through by exploring ways in which school organisation and practice can cater for a wider range of needs	Head teacher and senior managers are creating a common sense of purpose and are together exploring ways of promoting greater inclusion All staff are actively exploring strategies to provide greater access for all pupils	Head teacher, senior managers and governing body have a shared vision of the school's inclusive philosophy and practice All staff, including ancillary and support staff, share this vision and are actively involved in realising it in day to day practice
Environment	Access audit carried out – beginning to plan for implementation. School is beginning to plan for admission of pupils with a wider range of needs than at present Some staff influencing growing awareness of issues about inclusion	Staff aware of the need for display and ways in which it can be achieved, eg through the use of IT Some access-audit has been carried out and efforts have been made to adapt environment enabling more pupils to gain access Regular debate and awareness of inclusion issues demonstrated Positive attitudes towards SEN demonstrated across the school eg respect for all through the work of tutors, assemblies etc	All pupils aware that their work is valued. Individual achievements are recognized and celebrated IT used consistently and throughout the school Annual access audit carried out – review of environment to ensure that school is improving access to meet the targets it is setting Total access to the curriculum for a range of SEN to all members of the community All members of school community actively promote climate which values all school members
Collective Review	Some aspects of SEN provision have been audited Differences between groups have been audited eg boys, girls, ethnic groups	Teachers observe each other's practice to share and improve on specific strategies for SEN pupils School monitors progress of pupils with SEN Movement of pupils on the SEN register is monitored	Review of progress and achievement of SEN pupils incorporated into school review procedure Other groups monitored eg boys, ethnic groups Annual targets set for improvement of progress for pupils with SEN Success criteria within SEN policy includes eg reduction of numbers of pupils on SEN register Some work done with other school eg through cultural families of schools

Figure 10 continued

	Emergent	Established	Advanced
Staff Development	Staff training needs identified at whole school level Staff development programme for SEN linked to SDP is in place	There is an introduction programme for new staff which includes SEN/disability/Code of Practice Key staff, including SEN, learning support, pastoral and curriculum are identified and trained SDP identifies SEN training needs across a range of development targets	There is a structured training programme, including induction for new staff, linked to SDP and involving support services All staff, including teacher and non-teaching receive training about SEN which is audited and reviewed regularly Key staff, ie Heads Of Dept and Curriculum leaders take initiative SEN training needs in all areas and for all staff eg pastoral and curriculum identified through SDP, monitored and reviewed annually
Parental and Community Involvement	Some involvement – parents encouraged to attend meetings School is seeking ways in which parents can be involved SENCOs report to parents about progress of pupils with SEN	Fully involved in supporting and reviewing progress Built into school procedures Use made of adults and other children to provide role models Some links with disability groups are beginning to be established Wide range of services eg LEA, Health, Social Services used to support knowledge, understanding, provision in the school	More structured approach to provide role models Environment and facilities are fully accessible to people with disabilities Partnership with community groups to promote inclusion School seeks views of under-represented groups School demonstrates practical understanding of wide range of support services Key staff have a well-developed knowledge about kind of support they can call on

Figure 10 continued

inclusion as a final state, and there are lots of steps, you can get more and more inclusive, and I suppose being totally inclusive you'll take anyone and everyone and work with them . . .'

'I think we are in a strange position where the legislation around special needs does create a culture of segregation within schools. You know that whole business of resources for children with statements creates those sort of problems. . . . But one of the things I try to do here is to move that on a bit and to get away from thinking about particular groups of children and to think about all children as having educational needs . . . I've used the language of special needs in the 'Standard' because that's what we're working with . . . I don't think we've got it right over special needs at all. The difficulties we have with resources and statementing cause huge problems for us. If you could get rid of them it would solve half our problems straight away. And there are conceptual problems around the labels we give children and we're still caught up in that. I'd love to get away from all that.'

Considerable resources went into the piloting of the 'Standard for Inclusive Education' in eighteen mainstream and two special schools in 1997. The scheme was not designed for the segregated sector, but the advisor welcomed the participation of these two schools because 'a) they need to know what is going on and b) there may be some useful things that can be developed in conjunction with mainstream schools'. The LEA supported half-day training sessions on how to respond to the materials and cover for staff to spend time researching the practice in their schools, advisors visited the schools, and the University of Birmingham ran a linked course on issues of inclusion and exclusion. After the pilot stage it was expected that all schools would use the 'Standard' and that they would do this without the additional support. However, even after what the advisor describes as 'intensive support', there was a noticeable variation between schools in their ability to arrive at a workable action plan, making it unlikely that the scheme would be continued.

For a project to have a lasting impact on a school it requires the support of the head teacher and other senior members of staff. As the advisor said:

It depends on the quality of the people you've got. If you've got a good representative . . . who is well regarded in the school, that will have an impact on the direction that the school is able to take . . . if you've got support within the school there will be change.

This was not the case with this particular pilot school. Yet undertaking activities in relation to the 'Standard' was seen as positive by a number of the pilot schools because it had increased the level of communication within and between schools. The advisor told us about a pilot secondary school in which the 'Standard' had 'really galvanized staff into thinking about particular areas they hadn't really thought about before', and three small nursery schools with similar targets had worked on the project together. So the 'Standard' has acted as a catalyst for a range of initiatives, even if the formal tasks required were not accomplished easily.

Inspecting Birmingham LEA

Birmingham was one of the first LEAs to be inspected by the Office for Standards in Education (OFSTED), as part of a pilot project carried out in conjunction with the Audit Commission. The inspection took place in October 1997, and the Report was published in January 1998. The commentary begins: 'This is a very well-run LEA . . . in important respects, the performance of the LEA as an organisation exceeds that of other LEAs OFSTED has inspected' (OFSTED 1998: 3).

The report shows that attainment levels remain lower than the national average but that the rate of improvement is well above that for authorities with similar populations of students. It acknowledges that:

> [The CEO] has had an enormous impact. He has the ability to articulate a very particular educational vision and to inspire teachers to new levels of commitment. His accessibility to schools is much appreciated. The LEA would not have made anywhere near as much progress without his leadership.
>
> (p.4)

However, there were crucial questions to be asked about the expression of the LEA's vision, the substance of its approach to school improvement and the match between the two. Schools defined 'improvement on previous best' in various different ways and they 'found ingenious ways to avoid confronting basic, central failures by celebrating progress that was at best modest and, very occasionally, entirely spurious' (p.22).

The Birmingham Advisory and Support Service (BASS) was the service identified by the inspectors as most concerned with raising standards and, after judging that their work with primary schools was better than that with secondary schools, they concluded: 'This is unequivocally a success and a key to the LEA's effectiveness' (p.31).

The section in the report on support for special educational needs refers neither to processes of inclusion and exclusion nor to mainstream and segregated schools. It praises the exclusions unit for its use of data collection and analysis and, in a later section, indicates that since the Unit was set up the number of permanent exclusions (around 12 per cent of all exclusions) has fallen, following a rise of 68 per cent between 1991 and 1996. The over-representation of Afro-Caribbean students has been reduced to under half the national rate, but not eliminated.

Raising the attainment levels of these students is a priority and, in a rare and indirect reference to inclusive values, the report indicates how this can be achieved: 'In those schools where the strategies for improvement engage all pupils and where account is taken of the multi-ethnic nature of the school community, the performance of Afro-Caribbean pupils raises no specific concerns and they are doing well' (p.40). Otherwise, it appears that OFSTED is neutral on the question of underlying principles in its search for good practice and improved results. The publication of the report was accompanied by stories of the conflict between the CEO and the chief inspector, who criticized the city's approach as unclear and reluctant to face the facts about failing students and schools (see Bright 1998: 20).

Developing a policy for inclusive education

The city's approach to a policy for inclusive education can be traced through a series of pronouncements made during the 1990s. First of all, in an 'Education Development Strategy' statement of 1995, the chair of the Education Committee identified the following 'key values': 'A commitment to equality and access, partnership and quality' (Howell 1995: 1).

He then focused on four priority areas of work: information technology, the University of the First Age, LEA planning and special educational needs. The statement refers to progress, coordination, increased funding and effective management. The aim was for 'an efficient, targeted and responsive service', as 'a first step in the challenging task of ensuring that all SEN services provide the best possible value for money in supporting pupils with special educational needs' (ibid.: 3).

Second, the new division of special educational needs (SEN) produced a *Special Educational Needs Strategies Handbook*, also in 1995, in response to the 1993 Education Act and the 1994 Code of Practice. The *Handbook* includes a draft policy statement:

> (a) All children are entitled to a relevant and worthwhile education designed to enable individual pupils to participate fully in society and to contribute to, and benefit from it.
> (b) This education will normally be provided in a mainstream nursery, primary or secondary school, thus allowing participation in the local community and in home life with parents. Where this is not possible alternative special arrangements will be made in consultation with parents and where appropriate the young person.
>
> (*SEN Handbook* 1995: 1)

Provision was seen to include city mainstream schools, school-based units, off-site units and special schools, or provision in another LEA. As well as a commitment to quality, there was a commitment to the 'continued adjustment to the pattern of provision in order to respond to choices being made by parents and pupils' (ibid.: 1).

The principles underlying this statement 'are based on a policy of inclusion', though enrolment in the variety of mainstream provision is conditional, to be 'wherever possible' (ibid.: 2).

Third, the assistant director for SEN circulated a discussion paper 'On the development of inclusive education provision in the context of continuous schools improvement'. It refers to the city's Strategy 2000 and to the 'determination to help build inclusive communities in a city aspiring to a philosophy of equality of opportunity and success for everyone' (see SEN division 1996). The purpose of inclusion is described in terms of quality learning, value for money and exceeding legislative requirements. The purpose of the paper, which lists current provision in the city, other initiatives and concrete suggestions for development projects, was to engage all interested groups in practical planning, and its authors were conscious of the need to reassure staff working in segregated settings that their 'quality of professional opportunity' would not be compromised.

The next year, the SEN division issued an 'inclusion position statement', set out in note form as twenty-four bullet points. It represents a progress report on specific projects, for example the piloting of the 'Standards for Inclusion', the secondment of a community education teacher to the inclusion team (see Chapter 3), the opening of a mainstream primary resource base for children classified as having 'emotional and behavioural difficulties', governor training, attendance and exclusions targets and the planned relocation of two primary special schools to mainstream sites.

Fourth, in response to the government's legislation of 1997, the city's OFSTED report and a conference of local head teachers, a set of discussion papers was published in 1998 under the collective title *Achieving in Partnership*. One was the 'Strategic Plan for Inclusion'. Other topics included the overall education development plan, funding and, separated from the topic of 'inclusion', behaviour support. The Strategic Plan adopts the following definition: 'Inclusive Education removes the barriers that prevent children taking a full part in the life of the community. It tells *all* children that they are good enough to belong and have the right to belong' (City of Birmingham Education Department 1998: 3). However, it also states that 'along with mainstream schools, special schools play an equal and critical role in the development of inclusion within Birmingham.'

But:

> The role of special schools will need to change in response to a wide demand for [their] expertise. It is important that the Education Service capitalises on the sharing of skills between professionals. Inclusive education involves a commitment to every pupil. In this context, a network of services approach in which needed services support the pupil

rather than taking the pupil to the services, makes more sense than a continuum of placement approach, which presumes removal from the learning community.

(p.7)

No agreed Council policy followed the consultation period, and the inclusion team was replaced by the inclusion consultancy (see Chapter 3). The most recent city-wide initiative aimed at combating inequalities in education, the Birmingham Excellence in Cities Partnership, has not so far taken an active role in securing agreement to an explicit policy for inclusive education.

Excellence in the city of Birmingham 1999

Following the government's Excellence in Cities initiative (1999), the Birmingham Excellence in Cities (EiC) Partnership was established in 1999, comprising the city's ninety-two mainstream secondary schools and special schools with secondary-aged students. The overall aim is: 'To widen participation and raise achievement within the 16–19 cohort of students in schools and colleges' (Birmingham City Council Education Department 1999, Introduction).

To realize this aim, the city was divided into six 'networks' of secondary schools so that, as far as possible, within each one there would be a mix of poverty and wealth and thus comparability between them. Learning mentors have been appointed to individual schools, and within each area there is a learning support centre (LSC) with a 'pre-exclusion' focus and a city learning centre (CLC) with a focus on hi-tech curriculum development, in what's called a 'hub and spoke' model. Like the University of the First Age, therefore, the partnership schools would be involved in providing learning experience for students in a variety of settings, mobilizing both students and resources. However, although the CLCs seem to be operating as they were intended, providing for students across the cluster of partner schools though actually based in one of them,

> it's less clear that that's the case for the LSCs, because secondary schools were reluctant to be seen to be dumping grounds for difficult pupils, so although they have an outreach capacity, they actually deal, largely, with the pupils within their own school. Not entirely satisfactory solution.
> (Advisor, Birmingham EiC Partnership)

Up to ten per cent of the students in a school can be identified as gifted and talented and the EiC Partnership would be supporting clusters of schools to collaborate in providing enrichment activities for them. When I asked about the consequences of this additional mechanism for selection in the city, the Partnership advisor said there was 'no big dilemma', because it was about 'how you develop access to learning for individual pupils . . . how you meet their particular needs. . . . It's about fulfilling the potential of individual pupils'.

The advisor argued that there was no direct link to social class or wealth because the students who were identified in one school or area would not be the same as those identified in another. He argued that the initiative was about 'underachievement' and 'in that sense it's quite in line with the overall philosophy of tackling social exclusion'.

The issue of what geographical unit to use as a basis for inter-school or inter-agency cooperation emerged as a theme of the conversation I had with the Partnership advisor. Statutory Education Action Zones (EAZs), which were outside the control of the LEAs, experienced difficulties with funding and bureaucracy and the government is planning to merge them within their Excellence in Cities frameworks. In Birmingham, where there are two EAZs, there are also six non-statutory Small Education Action Zones (SEAZs), which focus on one secondary school and its main feeder primaries. The catchment area of a secondary school is, like the Neighbourhood Renewal areas, based on a political ward, even though in practice students may come from a much wider area. Not only that, but the boundaries of housing, education, health and social services areas do not coincide, which makes collaborative funding arrangements difficult. Also, the relationship between education and housing has become more complicated recently, as the number of social housing groups has increased. The advisor argued that, in any case, basing services on a fixed geographical unit may not be in the best interests of users:

> My misgiving is that they're seen as developing things within the ward, within the ward. . . . To my mind the real focus of the ward should be how you facilitate people actually getting there [to the city centre] rather than thinking you can replicate that [city centre amenities] in every ward.

DISCUSSION

An incredible amount of activity was generated by the new chief education officer's arrival in the city, and during the 1990s Birmingham became a focus for national and international attention. Priorities for educational services included: multi-agency collaboration, joint funding arrangements, early childhood health, support networks for practitioners and projects (community- and school-based) aimed at reducing disadvantage. Developments relating to processes of inclusion and exclusion reflect this re-energized and positive ethos. However, it was not possible to secure agreement to a clear and coherent city-wide policy.

Birmingham's approach to inclusion and exclusion has consisted of several separate strands. First, there's the special educational needs perspective represented by commitments to quality, specialized services and value for money. Second, there's an equalities strand represented by a commitment to rights. Third, there's a perspective in which 'behaviour' is separated from 'learning' and, therefore, in which exclusion is sometimes separated from inclusion. It has not been possible to achieve a resolution of these differences and move towards a more coherent approach.

The different strands can be detected in a number of projects and initiatives. For example, implicit in the 'Standards for Inclusive Education' materials is a staged, linear, progress towards a final goal – an attainable state. There is no explicit definition of 'inclusive education' at the beginning, which makes it possible for two different approaches to be reflected at the same time: first, a deficit model in relation to individuals and, second, a more social approach to whole school cultures. The advisor who co-authored the materials acknowledges this but argues that the retention of the 'special needs' thinking is necessary because that is what shapes the allocation of resources. The materials do not therefore reflect his personal views.

This ambivalence results in a lack of clarity in the language of the 'Standards' which makes it hard for schools to respond. The statements under the heading of 'teaching and learning', for example, are difficult to assess. How could you 'measure', at the 'emergent' level, the meaning of 'some examples of curriculum approaches'? What constitutes an 'emergent' 'range of individual needs' compared to a 'wide range of individual needs' at the 'advanced' level? Could any school ever attain the 'advanced' level when statements are expressed in terms of absolutes, as in 'All teachers ensure that every individual need is catered for . . . '? However, using the 'Standards' did seem to increase the participation of staff, and they said they benefited from the opportunity for discussion. This implies that the evaluation of social processes requires discussion and the gathering of a range of perspectives rather than the filling in of matrices.

Draft policies for inclusive education originated from officers with a background in or explicit responsibility for special educational needs, who were structurally separated from those with responsibility for behaviour support and from those whose remit was equality. Policies were confused because of these inconsistencies and tensions. Chapter 3 looks at these complexities in more detail.

REFERENCES

Audit Commission (1994) *Seen but Not Heard: Coordinating Community Child Health and Social Services for Children in Need*, London: Audit Commission, Her Majesty's Stationery Office.

Beech, M. and Chinner, M. (2001) *Inclusion Networks* [Standards Fund 18B(1A)] 2000–2001. Evaluation Report, City of Birmingham Education Department.

Birmingham Advisory and Support Service (BASS) (1995) *School Improvement Butterflies Handbook*, Birmingham: BASS.

Birmingham Advisory and Support Service (BASS) (1996) *A Framework for Intervention*, Birmingham: BASS.

Birmingham City Council Education Department (1995) *Special Educational Needs Strategies Handbook*, Birmingham: Birmingham City Council.

Birmingham Education Commission (1993) *Aiming (High* First Wragg Report), Birmingham: Education Department.

Birmingham Education Commission (1995) *Hitting the Target?* (Second Wragg Report), Birmingham: Education Department.

Bright, M. (1998) 'Row Flares as Schools Report is Rewritten', *Observer*, 18 January 1998.

Department for Education and Employment (DfEE) (1999) *Excellence in Cities*, London: DfEE (Green Paper).

Howell, A. (1995) *A Great Learning City*, Birmingham: Birmingham City Council Education Committee Paper.

Office for Standards in Education Audit Commission (1998) *Inspection of Birmingham Local Education Authority*, London: OFSTED.

Schoon, N. (2001) *The Chosen City*, London: Spon Press.

Social Exclusion Unit (2001) *A New Commitment to Neighbourhood Renewal*, National Strategy Action Plan, London: Social Exclusion Unit.

Upton, C. (1998) Information sheet on the IKON Gallery.

Chapter 3

Perspectives on inclusion/ exclusion in Birmingham

Patricia Potts

INTRODUCTION

Perspectives on developments in the city's educational services since the early 1990s are provided in this chapter by the then chair of the elected Council's Education Committee, the chief education officer, the deputy chief education officer (who had been the city's first assistant director for special educational needs), the new assistant director for special educational needs, a primary school head teacher, a secondary school head teacher, the inclusion team leader, the head of the exclusions unit and two members of a special school outreach team. Some were at the beginning of their professional life in the city, while others had long experience in a variety of roles. We talked to the outreach teachers together but otherwise spoke to people individually. Their opinions give us a many-sided view of what inclusive education has meant in Birmingham, both as the aim of policy and as the culture of practice.

Defining 'inclusion'

We asked our participants to give us their definition of inclusion and their responses run as a thread through the whole of this chapter. But here are two examples to start our exploration of the views of the city's insiders. The chair of the elected Council's Education Committee was alone among our interviewees in drawing on the principle of 'comprehensive' education:

> 'We feel that there are a number of issues around equity [that] are important to us and we need to make sure that every youngster has the full opportunity to take advantage of all the facilities that we can offer them and there is a feeling that separate education sometimes, for some youngsters, doesn't offer them the full facilities that others get. It is a comprehensive principle. . . . We think that if possible youngsters should be educated together, in the same institutions. A secondary, but quite important motivation behind this is for the youngsters who don't have any special need having daily contact with those who do. . . . There are

those two elements really, for those youngsters who we believe shouldn't be segregated and for youngsters to come across a whole range of other young people.'

The chief education officer's approach to inclusion derived from his aim of responding to individual learning styles:

'If you were with a mainstream school and you were pushing them towards school improvement, you would say: "Are you in favour of success for all the kids or for some of the kids?" I mean, the practice is that most of our system is in favour of some of the kids and not all of the kids. So I would explore with people: "Well, if you are in favour of success for all of the kids rather than some, then that does mean . . . accommodating to individual differences." It means having a view of intelligence which is multiple rather than general. It means accepting people who develop at different paces. It challenges you. . . . It changes the way you organise things. Accommodating kids, making it much easier for them to be included, whatever their barriers to learning may be. I think that is the fundamental argument.'

Perspectives on developing a policy

The chief education officer told us this story about his experience of inclusion and exclusion in the city:

'Shortly after I came I went to a series of meetings in the evening with governors and I used overheads where I was pitching about what principles I stood for, and one of them was for an inclusive, not exclusive. . . . I pitched them into opposites, inclusive and exclusive system . . . and I explained what I meant. As a whole we are going to try and have a society which accommodates as far as it possibly could, so that everybody could be more or less within their community and respected for their different talents and that, if that was the case, then there will be implications about the way we organise schooling and indeed the way any school operated. . . . And I have to say I didn't think it was an inclusive city. In education, anyway, though actually, curiously enough, in terms of its wider cycle in history . . . you know of all the cities, it has done pretty well in taking people from very, very different backgrounds. It's a short history. But we had a selective school system and that was not particularly helpful. . . . When there was that brief history, in the late sixties, early seventies, where the mode was to have villages for different special educational needs built together on campuses, they took the opportunity to build the schools in that way. With the benefit of hindsight I don't think that was a very clever thing to have illustrated because I am absolutely sure that that meant that people knew where I was coming from . . . and I say no, these things have to evolve. It takes time, people need to look at different practice, discuss what is possible and then adjust their practices. You can't legislate for people to think in different ways, they have to come to think in different ways because they have observed different practice and it works and it stimulates their information and they have to have a debate about their values and it's not a thing you can legislate for. . . . So these debates were happening then and I met principally audiences such as special school heads who were deeply concerned that I had a kind of plan in my back pocket . . . I was pretty engaged in trying to work within the mainstream to adjust their practices into being more inclusive and less exclusive and devoted a lot of time to that and kept hammering the principles and their adoption . . . I was pushing school improvement.'

About eighteen months later, a new assistant education officer (AEO) was appointed, whose background was in special educational needs. (During the period of our research she became deputy chief education officer and line manager of a new assistant director for special educational needs.) The chief education officer continued:

'She came in and talked inclusion and talked inclusion and talked inclusion . . . and I would say over the course of the next eighteen months she shifted people's debate and people were beginning to think that, well, inclusion was probably quite a good idea . . . [She] was pursuing ideas of if we did begin to change . . . the pattern of schooling so that there were special provision within or alongside [the mainstream] then what would that mean for health services and how would we work with them and she had got some joint funding going and then I reckon we lost oomph. . . . She went into hospital and it had been heavily dependent on her . . . the whole thing lost momentum.'

Has any further progress been made?

'But the system, don't forget, was inhabited, when I arrived. The system was inhabited in all the support services by separatists. Not by people who were pro-inclusion. Now the difference is that those systems are inhabited and led by people who are pro-inclusion. So in the sense of the plumbing of the place, the plumbing of the place is much more inclusive than it was. When I arrived I was literally alone in talking about inclusion.'

The assistant education officer agreed that attitudes have changed:

'Going round the city now, the feel about the way people talk about inclusion is completely different to the way it was when we first met, when we first started talking about it. . . . Now people are sitting forward to talk about inclusion as opposed to the body language that [says] "That might be the policy but you can count me out. I don't want anything to do with it". . . . Although there is still concern, it's not fear any more.'

However, her perception of initial attempts to put inclusion on the agenda was rather different:

'I think we have been relatively successful at associating inclusion with school improvement and getting away from where it started, which was a separate . . . strategy, but I think we dragged it back into the main agenda. It started kind of being drifted out as being a special needs strategy. . . . I think it was seen at that stage as being an SEN issue. . . . It was the SEN division driving it, that it was me driving it. That it was a little bit haywire, a little bit loose. A little bit too visionary, too little strategic and too little backed up with resource and commitment and all of those things. So even though we had a committee paper for [a] policy [on] inclusion, even though we had Strategy 2000 [aimed at increasing the number of students with statements of special educational needs in mainstream schools] . . . even though we had me going round, standing on platform after platform after platform talking about inclusion, it was still marginal.'

Later in our conversation, however, the AEO returned to the early struggles to get inclusion debated and now presented a view more in accord with that of the CEO:

'Within minutes of arriving in the city he had let it be known that he had an inclusion [agenda] . . . He came in with a kind of banner over his head of school improvement. . . . He set up his store of doing away with special schools and making sure all schools improved sufficiently to be able to provide for everybody that lived in their locality. So his integration theme was not just about special needs, it was about ethnic minority children. It was about culture. . . . When I arrived, because I have a background in special needs, I sought to temper that because I felt that he was going at it like a bull in a china shop and we were simply going to set up barriers that we would find almost impossible to shift. . . . So I started with my charm offensive within the special schools sector itself. Going around and talking to people, talking about the importance of main-taining what was good in that and saying that what we were not trying to do was to undermine special education but simply to make sure that special education could be delivered in more places than it was being delivered at the moment and that we still needed the expertise and the knowledge and the skills and so on and that what we wanted to do was kind of break down the barriers that existed around special schools and to make them more of a resource for the city.'

The AEO also worked closely with mainstream school governors, many of whom are elected city council members. This enabled her to discuss the development of Council policy as well as school improvement in practice. A change of chair of the Education Committee made a positive difference, in her view, but not enough to secure an agreed Council policy on inclusion:

'The chair of education when I arrived . . . wasn't really interested in special needs. He was interested in school improvement but he didn't feel inclusion was part of that. When [he left] there was a completely different feel about it because [his successor] was a very child-centred person, had been a teacher and really wanted to push the special needs agenda and she joined forces with me and said: "OK, let's get this now on to the city council agenda and make it into a policy statement." So we took a draft policy statement to the committee. It got talked out. . . . They wouldn't move beyond draft . . . because they were being lobbied all the time by all the self-interest groups about: "You can't afford it. It will cost you millions . . . There will be campaigns and none of you will be re-elected next year. It's too big a risk." And so we settled for a draft policy as part of our SEN handbook and I have to say to you that it is still draft, as we speak. That policy statement is still draft.'

The new assistant director for special educational needs had been in Birmingham for a few months when we spoke to her. She saw the mobilization of existing resources as a key feature of the city's inclusion policy:

'It's making the most of the resources that we have got, the philosophy of school improvement and also the idea of collaboration between schools, seem to be three very strong themes, which are the central strategy of the policy. So the idea of moving towards inclusion networks where there are groups of schools who we will develop, with them, in partnership with them, the capability and the capacity to meet the needs of the children in their community, within that group of schools. Linked to that is the notion, almost a dating agency notion . . . looking at schools which have the specialist providers and looking at how they can link in with mainstream providers to then become an inclusive school, which again is making the most of resources and knowledge wherever we have it.'

However, she also saw that:

'There is a lack of clarity, which surprises me in some ways, and I actually think that that's been influenced by the politics, the reality of the politics of working with a very, very diverse group of people . . . people who have got different vested interests. I mean, I wasn't here, but I can see the trademarks of [the CEO] coming in, very inclusive, totally inclusive, and then how that has become softened and in some ways is used by some, I think, to avoid inclusion.'

The exclusions unit

Following the 1996 Education Act, Birmingham experienced a huge increase in requests for statements of special educational needs, both for students whose learning requirements were not met and for those who were excluded on disciplinary grounds, all of which were, at that time, processed by one casework team within the SEN division. The exclusions unit was created to share this overload, a move which the head of the unit admits was more about 'protecting the interests of the team' than about any 'vision'. However:

'When they made [my] appointment, it was really a blank sheet of paper, so the fact that I was a teacher and therefore wanted to do much more of a management than an administrative [job], which is what it could have been, they left me to do it, which I greatly appreciated. So we were able to develop the way we managed the process, much more interactively with schools and as they gained confidence in the way that we managed the process, they began to talk to us a lot more about how they could avoid it [exclusion].'

Like some of her colleagues, the head of the exclusions unit understands the city's inclusion policy in terms of cultural change:

'[Exclusion] has reduced again, massively compared to what it was when I started. But I don't think that has got anything to do with exclusion, that reduction. I think that has been more about a change of culture here, which has enabled it to be approached from the opposite end because I think if you set out to reduce exclusion, you are setting yourself a much harder and more complex task than if you set out to improve schools and raise achievement. . . . I think there is real evidence that many of these initiatives have been very successful.'

She is critical of the draft policy document, however: 'I suppose my lasting memory of it is the minimal reference to the greatest difficulty. . . . I am dealing with the bit that is hardest to include . . . the EBD [students identified as having 'emotional or behavioural difficulties].'

She believes that 'The kind of relationship we develop with our schools, through the exclusion process, has done as much to promote inclusion in the city as almost anything else and the reduction in the exclusion figures, I think, supports that view.' (In 2000, the target was 280 and in fact 278 students were excluded; see also Thornton 1999.)

But reducing exclusion from schools was only a part of what the head of the unit saw as her job. Two situations in which students had had to be excluded, both involving violence – one in connection with a criminal racket and one following a traumatic bereavement – were given to us to illustrate how difficult it is for schools to maintain a no-exclusions policy and to discuss the importance of what happens next:

> 'I had a conversation with somebody in the authority a few weeks ago who began . . . by telling me how opposed they were to any form of exclusion. And then I said 'OK, then. We have got one head teacher who has discovered that she is presiding over an extortion group, that there is a park near her, with a hole in the tree, which the kids are using to store weapons. And when kids don't give the money by the normal means, they go to the park, retrieve the weapons and hold a gun to their head. That is a scenario. What would you do? You know, you have got parents who are coming round the school and saying, "What are you going to do?" But . . . if you are standing there with a gun to your head, you don't worry too much whether it is real or loaded, especially if you are a child. What would you do? And that person said, "Well, I suppose there are exceptions when you would exclude." You'd have to, you know. And that's the kind of conversation we have all the time . . .

> 'The kid last year who was walking home from school, it's not the easiest of schools, not the easiest of areas, not the easiest of kids, but walking home from school, aware in front of him of the problem with the tower block he was walking towards. Gets nearer, the problem is obviously very serious, there is an ambulance, a fire engine. Gets closer and as he arrives at the tower block there is a woman on the roof who jumps and it's his mother. Now that kid has to deal with that and the way he dealt with it was to be extremely angry. And that anger was coming out in school and he clearly needed counselling, clearly needed help and tried to access it but before they were successful in accessing it, a teacher dealt with something, probably slightly insensitively and the kid hit him and knocked him out and you had an unconscious teacher on the classroom floor. Now the fact that you and I understand where that came from, the fact that the school was aware and was trying to get help, didn't alter the fact that the kid had knocked out a teacher in front of a class and was in danger of hitting out at everybody else . . . and the only way the school could protect itself, in terms of looking after the safety of everybody else, was to exclude that child from the school.'

To try and develop support in the spaces between schools the head of the exclusions unit advocates collaboration between departmental divisions and between education and other statutory agencies, such as housing and health.

'We are being helped enormously by relaxing some of the requirements . . . that enable the curriculum to be more flexible for, especially, Key Stage 4, to begin to look at a variety of provision that enables the child to have some time in the centre [learning support centre], some time at [further education] college, some time on work experience [and] those children with examination potential can still do them. . . . There are some very positive things happening about keeping Key Stage 4 kids in the system without necessarily returning to mainstream school . . . the potential for returning to a more kind of sharing culture, with kids going in and out of different venues perhaps or being able to link [activities] through technology.'

However, it is impossible for the head of the unit to ignore the tensions that have arisen since moving towards inclusion has been put on the agenda:

'You see the strides that schools are trying to make to include all children but you come head-on with the tension that that creates. . . . There is a difficulty from parents demanding the difficult children are removed. The difficulty of trying to have a consistent, fairly applied, behaviour policy in school, the difficulty of trying to include all children when everything schools are going to be judged on is competitive in terms of league tables and the attainment of all the other children. . . . I mean, even [the CEO] has gone to press in supporting a school that made the headlines over bullying and his first paragraph was talking about the very quick investigation and response the school had made, including the exclusion on the day it happened. So that's all right then. By the time you go through the rest of his letter and you are at the last paragraph, it's about the value of the inclusive system and keeping all our children in schools. There are two sentences in the letter, one in the first paragraph and one in the last which, for me, just summed up the tension that we feel.'

Views from a primary and a secondary school

The primary head teacher we talked to saw the city's inclusion policy as 'muddled':

'I think the confusion is over league tables, improving on previous best, on resources, about how to actually tackle the fact that at some point there has got to be a stop, in order to start again and a muddle about how they are going to find a way through that sea. It's not about the actual vision at the end. I think there is a vision at the end and I think it's not totally clear but I think it is about including as many children as possible in the local schools and ideally it would be about all children in their local schools. . . . I think Birmingham wanted inclusion but I don't think there was a particular will to move forward very quickly. I think there were so many other initiatives and I think that this one is such a sticky one that it was one they maintained by a thread . . . I feel that Birmingham back-pedalled, if not back-pedalled, they sort of marked time.'

Despite the absence of a clear and dynamic policy, however, this head teacher does think that there has been constructive change for her school:

'Inclusion for us enabled us to have a better staffing ratio, staff who were far better tuned into children's needs, not just special needs but all needs, and enabled us to improve the environment and the learning capacity for all on site, not just for the children but for the staff as well. I had involved the SENCO [special educational needs coordinator] in every curriculum working group. . . . By including you take more notice of outside practice and everything you do, you think, you might consciously think "Is that inclusive?" There are certain things that you do and I have to stop myself because I think: "No, if I do that, it's actually excluding somebody else or that will mean that someone else won't have access to that." I think the ethos itself is an improvement because you are always going back and examining, trying to make better opportunities. . . . Most of the groups I go to now, there is a greater representation and a much better valuing of the people who are talking, which I feel is good. . . . It is great to hear people talking about valuing people who for years have been treated like dogsbodies.'

Nevertheless there are children whose inclusion in her school could not be sustained:

'[We had] a little girl who had severe delay in all sorts of areas, was a very big child for seven, was just beginning to learn and just be able to control a pencil and being able to make meaningful marks, and she loved life here but we felt that she needed to begin to learn through her senses. At three, she had had to start again as a baby and nobody knew what her potential was going to be. . . . We saw her all the way through until the end of Year 2 but we felt she . . . needed touch, she needed to go into water, she needed a swimming pool, she needed to be able to go into a ball area and be able just to push and bang around, which she did do in the playground but other children were on the end of her arms and other children loved her . . . but she actually went to . . . a local special school. . . . We couldn't give her the same sort of environment. . . . Maybe we will be able to in the future, but for her at that moment she needed these environmental stimuli which we couldn't give. . . .

'One child I am thinking of particularly, he was just so difficult to manage by the time we got him to Year 2, he would bite . . . and he would hit and he would kick for no apparent reason. You wouldn't know what set him off and we tracked it, the psychologist tracked it and we did all sorts of things. He had a statement. When he was very little, if he went into a tease, you just knew, everybody just left him where he was and if he was going to kick the wall or lie down and scream, the children just carried on round him, you know, "Oh gosh, he's at it again!", and when he would finish, someone would walk over to him and [say] "OK, go and sit down". . . . He had better times and worse times, and his mum said, "Oh, I was just like this when I was a child." . . . She split up with a partner, who came back into school because he had a lot to do with the little boy, and he said, "If you had known her when she was a young child, you would know just why he is why he is." . . . By the time he had got to Year 2, he had become destructive and the assistant who worked in the class – I mean she loved him, she took him right the way through – and one afternoon he beat her on the neck and punched her as well and she came across and she was shaken. She just looked at me and said, "I hate him." She said, "Until today I have loved him and now I just hate him." And I said, "That's it, you can't work with him again". . . . And I excluded him, really to make the point and to give the class a break because the class had had it up to here and the teacher had had it up to here and that is where you feel a failure. But what more can we do? . . . You examine the structure in the classroom, you examine the environment, you examine all the other children. The other children were so good with him and he used to hurt them so horribly . . . I used to get parents in and "What are you going to do about this child?" '

The community served by this primary school 'varies from rich to some of the lowest deprivation in Birmingham. Socially, there is a huge number of single-parent families.' About a quarter of the children come from ethnic minority families and 43 per cent have free school meals (fewer than those who are entitled to them). The head teacher only accepts children from the local area, and this commitment led to developing the school's capacity to respond to them all. This school was involved in the Supported Places Initiative and, in 2000, was the only mainstream school (along with five special schools) to receive substantial funding as a lead school in an 'inclusion network' (see Chapter 2).

We also spoke to the head teacher of a secondary school of about 700 'poor white working-class' students, 60 per cent boys, including fifty-five young people with statements of special educational needs who experience speech and language difficulties. They are bussed in to the school each day from a wider catchment area than the other students. They used to be educated in a separate special unit but are now registered as one mainstream class in each year group. Most of them are still taught in discrete groups, which are much smaller than the average class. (See also Booth and Armstrong 1993). In the following autumn, the incoming Year 7 (around 140 students) will include twenty students with statements. About 20 per cent of the students come and go during the year, which is high for a secondary school and reflects the fact that the school has empty places, making it possible for students to come and go (see also Chapter 8). Fifty per cent of the students have free school meals. An independent boys' grammar school is 'up the road' and a large state girls' school is 'down the road'.

> 'We have now got 95 per cent of our kids leaving with one or more GCSEs. Now if you compare that to many schools in the city, that is really high. We are in the A bracket on value-added for that and we have got a very low-achieving population. So I would argue that that shows we are including all the children we have got here. We have got 80 per cent getting five A–Gs and 20 per cent getting A–Cs. Well even on the A–C that is C value-added and the A–Gs is a B. So I think we are doing pretty well really. Hopefully we are continuing to go up.'

This head teacher saw the city's inclusion policy as:

> '[enabling] most children to attend the local school and enabling schools to feel that they are capable of meeting the needs of most children. The dilemma comes [with] the most challenging group, "EBD". Everybody is nervous . . . and that is where I think they just want reassurance that all off-site provision isn't going to be closed down.'

We asked him if he thought it was possible to support all students within the mainstream.

> 'No, I don't. I don't think it would necessarily be right to. It does depend on the need of individual children. . . . I think it is possible to include far more than we have done in the past and that the majority of children would be able to. Whether they could attend their local school is, I think, a different matter and there is a lot of finance and practicalities around that.'

However, he sees a definite change and that this is positive:

> 'I think the culture is certainly changing and I suppose one of the most noticeable areas really is special education, which I think in some cases

has been hauled, screaming, into sort of the same concerns about achievement and quality of teaching, which is a huge shift, which is wonderful. The support from the top for that is very obvious. . . . They have done a lot on setting up groups and negotiating and talking and there has been more support for pupils in mainstream with statements, although it is a never-ending demand, isn't it, and now you have to look at it and say, "Is it actually cost-effective?" But that has happened. I suppose it's a cultural shift more than anything.'

The view from a special school

For some years before the new chief education officer arrived in Birmingham, one of the special schools for disabled children and young people was running an outreach service for the growing numbers of students in the mainstream. The service, now well established, is 'unique' in the city in that it is a school-based support service but funded centrally. This gives the teachers autonomy, credibility and access to a multi-professional team but it also isolates them from other support services in the city.

The outreach teachers' approach to inclusion was shaped by their commitment to the provision of an expert service from a centre of excellence:

'There is a lot of expertise in a place like this. . . . I see, personally, a huge number of advantages being based here. . . . Just our credibility, that we are actually teachers here. . . . At the end of last week there was a lot of publicity about us becoming a Beacon school and the schools that I have been into this week say "Oh". I think people look at us as being a real centre of expertise here. Not just two teachers with expertise but a real centre that they can call upon.'

Her colleague agreed:

'While there is a greater number of learning support assistants, integration assistants, who are not trained teachers, out in schools and [though] training is increasing for them . . . and there are some very good people doing very good jobs, there are some who have very little background and yet in many cases they are being expected to write their own curriculums for some of these children, whereas in schools like this . . . there are staff with the expertise.'

The special school where the teachers are based is one of three similar schools in the city, two of which have secondary departments. At one time

'[We] were taking children from the locality and they were children really right through a cross-section of intellectual levels as well as their motor-developmental problems but . . . within the last five years [our] roles have been redefined . . . we are taking the more sort of mainstream curriculum type . . . while [another school] on the other side of the city may be taking more on the developmental side. So therefore our children are often bussed right from the other side of the city, especially in secondary . . . Children are coming from a long long way now.'

Teachers from the three schools meet regularly: 'We have been able to share concerns and share resources and information. So that has been very beneficial and has, I suppose, given us more of a feeling of belonging.'

Since the 1994 Code of Practice, the outreach team has been doing much more inservice training in mainstream schools:

'That was a watershed really . . . schools are much better equipped to meet the need of those children on the early stages of the Code and then they will call us in when they need more specific expertise, so that our role has changed from working with the children to more of an advisory role.'

The outreach teachers work with a large number of children in a number of different schools, but they work most closely with two local primary schools, designated as 'satellites' for the special school (there is no local secondary 'satellite' school). Most children in this area are therefore placed in the mainstream right from the start, another reason why the children and young people at the special school come from further away.

One of the teachers described their outreach work with children as a combination of target setting and raising children's self-esteem:

'We have got a "tree of knowledge" where we are taking children to look at what they have previously been able to do and to target that in green. . . . From that, all pupils will sit and discuss what they have achieved. . . . Then to go on to having a look at what they actually want to achieve this term and it could be behaviour or their motor skills. It could be anything within literacy. It could be done as an individual, a group or as a class. . . . One school we went to, within the assembly hall, they hadn't just got trees of knowledge, they had forests.'

The teachers have also developed a series of subject-based '20 Hot Tips' handouts for secondary school teachers of students with a physical disability, saying: 'We felt that this was a way of getting inclusion started in a very sort of user-friendly type of way, without taking up much time and money, either from the mainstream school or here.'

Of the schools that call on them infrequently, the outreach teachers say:

'When you go [in], you start talking about inclusion, you could just get the feeling that they are not really at all turned on to it because it is actually a very minor thing in the grand scheme of what they are all having to jostle with in education at the moment.'

The inclusion team

During our time in the city, we have worked with several colleagues who were attached to the inclusion team. In the mid 1990s there was one officer working within the Education Department as the integration development coordinator. You have seen from the accounts of the CEO and AEO that they both feel their initial attempts to introduce moves towards inclusion were ill-judged. An informal discussion group, chaired by one of the senior officers, was convened specifically to bring together practitioners with widely differing views and the minutes were circulated to all schools and support services by the coordinator. No clear commitments emerged from this group, which did not have a specific remit or task and meetings ceased after about six months. However, the team of officers was expanded: a teacher was seconded from a primary school to work within schools on projects for promoting inclusive practices and the head of a mainstream unit for students identified as having speech and language difficulties was appointed to represent experience in secondary schools. After one term, he returned to his school, where the special unit was restructured into a series of mainstream year groups (see the secondary head teacher's interview, above).

The three-person inclusion team began working on a strategy for promoting inclusive practice across the department as a whole. The team of three practitioners and an administrator was expanded when one of the two new advisors for special educational needs was appointed as team leader. He was responsible for completing the draft inclusion strategy, Achievement in Partnership. While this strategy was out for consultation, however, he moved on to another authority. He was replaced by a special school head teacher but she also soon moved on to another post and was succeeded, in turn, by an educational psychologist.

The position of the inclusion team was never formalized and its members did not share a common perspective on their role. Some felt unsupported at divisional level. One team member said:

'My idea [of inclusion] and what is talked about bear no relation. They're still being ever so careful not to upset special schools. . . . It constantly gets watered down. . . . All schools need to change . . . but the talk of "transforming schools" and linking this to inclusion, common a couple of years ago, has declined.'

Another team member said:

> 'A philosophy of inclusion and a structure for change [are] kept separate.
> . . . Inclusive thinking is not embedded in practice. It's "out there", a
> distant concept. . . . My job is about consciousness-raising but this is in
> contradiction of the culture of those who appointed me.'

She told us that officers wanted to avoid confrontation, to achieve 'change
without pain', but that there was a catch–22 situation: people don't want
to be told what to do, but if there is no direction from the top people are
annoyed by the lack of clarity. The CEO 'had been successful' in putting
inclusion on people's agendas but that was as far as it went. This colleague
remembered the dynamic of the discussion group meetings as gender-
dominated, with the men gossiping together until the women called them to
order. The social relationships cut across the professional commitments
represented, precluded any head-on debate and, therefore, progress towards
an agreed policy.

The teacher secondments were not renewed, and the original coordinator
returned to full-time teaching in a secondary school. The team has been
renamed the inclusion consultancy service and explicitly located within the
special education needs division. There are three members of staff: the
educational psychologist as head, an administrative officer and a 'strategic
manager'. The introduction to the service on its website says:

> We are . . . responsible for shaping and developing the Education Service
> policy for inclusion and for disseminating the relevant policy documents
> and guidelines. . . . We believe that every child and young person should
> have an equal opportunity and right to: attend a local mainstream early
> years setting/school with appropriate resources and support networks,
> if that is the parents'/carers' preference (see: www.bgfl.org/services/
> inclus/).

The work of the inclusion consultancy implies a gradual transformation of
schools but within the existing pattern of overall provision.

Barriers to inclusion

A number of barriers to inclusion have been referred to: the legacy of selective
schooling in the city, violence in schools, vested interests, initiative overload,
competitive examinations, compartmentalized thinking, fear, uncertain
leadership, public expense. The voices we have heard so far are not equally
committed to inclusion and their views are sometimes ambiguous. Here, I
am going to take a closer look at what they say about the nature of resistance
to inclusion in Birmingham.

The primary school head teacher gave me her list of barriers:

'The barriers you tend to come across are often practical. They do, I suppose, come back to money in the end . . . but I think there is a lot more about attitude rather than money and I think it is the accepting attitudes and the teaching of self-respect. . . . There were a lot of problems in the special needs department and the remit of [the inclusion team] was huge and it never actually focused down, so although we have got special needs advisors in the city, there wasn't really a focus on children in the mainstream . . . the focus was all wrong. . . . I still think a lot of people are saying: "What more is this for us? What more can we take on board? We are not going to do anything unless we get more money." . . . It's going to be a long, slow publicity and selling the success of an inclusive environment to people, I mean, it's not going to go down well with a lot of people.'
PP: 'Who?'
'A lot of the high-achieving schools.'

She went on to discuss transfer to secondary school:

'The children we have who have quite severe needs end up going to a special school for secondary, which is very sad because that means that they are no longer with all their mates.'
PP: 'What do you think would have to happen for them to be supported with their friends in the mainstream?'
'I think a big part of that is about changing the way that the secondary curriculum is organized. . . . It is going to have to become far more literacy-based.'

The chief education officer gave parental choice as the most serious barrier to inclusion:

'It is preference. That is the biggest virus. But it is fuelled by the way LMS [local management of schools] operates. LMS need not operate in the way it does . . . You can do modifications to LMS so that it wasn't so, in such a pronounced way, inclined towards exclusion.' (See also MacLeod 2001)

He also talked about 'deep down' resistance, saying: 'I am not going to shift [head of a special school]. I am never going to shift him. Never.'
Later, he revised this view:

'I will call his bluff. I bet you if I could achieve the removal of some of the special provision from that site and I brought to that site some

mainstream provision, he would change into being an inclusive practitioner. I really think he would.'

The CEO was conscious of the limits to what he, one person, could do:

> 'It's a time and energy trap. . . . If I tackle that issue [selection on the
> grounds of low or high attainment] it would be noble but I will make
> absolutely no progress. . . . If, on the other hand, I tackle birth to eleven
> and make everything I could possibly make inclusive and successful up
> to the age of eleven, I would do far more good in the time available in
> my life to me than I would by heading off like Don Quixote and tilting
> at the whole of this city.'

The chair of the Education Committee said that opposition to inclusion
was about jobs and a mentality:

> 'There has been a huge resistance . . . mainly from teachers, mainly from
> teachers in the special schools. . . . There is a friend of mine whose
> brother was severely autistic and he's a governor at a residential school
> for autistic secondary aged youngsters and . . . of course some of them
> are very separatist . . . they are some of the ones who are difficult to move
> in their thinking. . . . The thing that concerns me most is how slowly it's
> progressing. We have had this policy for five years . . . and it grinds on
> very slowly.'

The inclusion team leader whom we interviewed, an ex-special school head
teacher, reflected further on the effect of segregated schools on educational
reform in Birmingham:

> 'We must have the biggest special schools in the country, and that has
> got to be a big barrier because the people in those schools, not the
> teachers . . . so much and the assistants . . . but the people who are
> dependent on them for their livelihoods and I think if we could do one
> thing in this authority and take things forward it would be to say, "Look,
> we will do this but we will do it with no redundancies". . . . The second
> bit is a fear in mainstream about children who are going to pull their
> exam results down . . . children who they are not going to be able to cope
> with and don't see as being "their" children. These children flourish in
> special schools because they suddenly start believing in themselves again
> . . . and they grow in confidence. . . . I think one of the biggest things for
> mainstream is actually working with children with emotional and
> behavioural difficulties. . . . Because we have reasonably successful
> special schools there isn't the drive. . . . And I guess it's a lack of political
> pressure. . . . Estelle Morris stood and said to a large audience: "If

parents want special schools they can have them." . . . We don't have, and I find this quite astonishing, a body of parents who will help to drive it through.

She concluded:

'Politically people will always find ways of preventing things from happening if that is their mindset and if they are powerful people in the city. . . . You could name them on the fingers of one hand. . . . There will be powerful resistors from the special schools but also from certain mainstream schools, and what we have got to do is work with the others and then it shifts.'

DISCUSSION

We asked our interviewees to give us their definition of inclusion and relate this to what they saw as Birmingham's policy. Their accounts were given to us in language that revealed a varying set of assumptions and associations. Some people saw inclusion policy as emerging from a distinct professional world of 'special educational needs'. Others linked it to mainstream 'school improvement'. These differences in commitment and perspective are reflected in the difficulty education officers have had in securing an agreed and coherent policy for moving towards greater inclusion in mainstream education. They may also be reflected in the nature of the working relationships that we developed during our years in the city. While we enjoyed ongoing contacts with a range of colleagues and were received with generosity and interest by schools and colleges, it was not possible for the research team to maintain as active and supportive a role with policymakers as our initial plans for action research implied.

Processes such as selection into segregated grammar or special schools have been politically impossible to challenge in Birmingham – as elsewhere – and both kinds of school have a high status in the city. Indeed, in what was described as a 'charm offensive', considerable resources were devoted to moving the thinking of the special school sector. More than one of our participants compared their approach to that of a 'dating agency'. A consequence of this has been that the special schools have exerted some control over the inclusion agenda while the capacity of the mainstream to respond to increasingly wide groups of students remains underutilized.

The retention of segregated specialized services also corresponds to the current promotion of targeted services within the mainstream. The primary school and the secondary school whose head teachers spoke to us both use setting by ability. The raising of standards as measured by competitive test identifies 'failures' who can then receive targeted provision and be easily managed. Assessment is associated with sorting learners into homogeneous groups. Further, off-site services can also be seen as part of the elaboration of a system-wide network and so be linked with initiatives such as the University of the First Age, although their underlying principles are quite different.

Numerous barriers to inclusion have been listed, as have significant moves towards greater inclusion. There is no doubting that the ethos of state education in Birmingham has changed dramatically since the early 1990s and that reducing inequalities between learners is central to that change. Whether this is to be strengthened by processes of inclusion or processes of selection is a core debate in the city.

REFERENCES

Booth, T. and Armstrong, F. (1993) *Learning For All*, Unit 16, Open University Course 'Learning For All' (E242), Milton Keynes, Open University.

MacLeod, D. (2001) 'Perils of the School Run', *Guardian* 3 August 2001, p.19.

Thornton, K. (1999) 'Disturbed Pupils Labelled Naughty', *The Times Educational Supplement*, 19 Feb 1999. Article discusses a DfEE-funded research project carried out by the University of Birmingham. The report is entitled 'Emotional and Behaviour Difficulties in the Mainstream' (publication number RR90).

MOVING TOWARDS INCLUSION?

A project entitled Moving Towards Inclusion was funded by the city's Education Department. The definition of inclusion was the same as in the 'Strategic Plan for Inclusion', the consultation document published in 1998 (see Chapter 2): 'Inclusive education removes the barriers that prevent children taking part in the life of the community. It tells *all* children that they are good enough to belong and have the right to belong.'

Children and staff in one secondary school, four primary schools, one special school and a nursery school participated in a series of activities designed to explore their hopes for and fears of greater inclusion and develop their ideas for possible solutions. The first phase of the project consisted of discussions with children parents/carers and staff, awareness-raising sessions for children, staff and governors, developing practical teaching materials and establishing inter-agency links. The second phase would extend what had been learned in the first by arranging visits to each other's schools for children, parents/ carers and staff and encouraging both informal and formal links to develop. A third phase aimed to further people's understanding of difference and their appreciation of the value of difference and diversity within a school. Team teaching, shared training sessions, shared inter-agency planning and learning in another setting would be features of this stage. The overall aim was for people to feel confident about welcoming a wider range of learners into the mainstream and for the project's participants to maintain active, flexible and mutual support.

The materials produced for children were designed to help them understand difference and were divided into four areas: 'Special Me' was designed to boost children's self-esteem as the foundation for rewarding social and learning experiences; 'My Feelings' helped children to understand their own and others' emotions; 'Me and My Friends' focused on what the children looked for in a friend and how they behave with friends; and 'Understanding Disability/Celebrating Difference' encouraged the children to think positively about what makes people different.

There was also a set of materials for staff, parents/carers and governors looking at attitudes and legislation and encouraging participants to discuss situations of direct relevance to them. Members of staff compiled long lists of their hopes, fears and solutions. Here are some examples:

Hopes for inclusion

- Children will become more tolerant of difference;
- To be a 'community' school, as our title says;
- To raise awareness of the uniqueness of everyone and what we can learn from each other;
- That no family with a disabled child . . . needs to feel different/ excluded/isolated/unwelcome by their local community;
- What a great idea to have physically disabled children and those emotionally disabled children . . . included. It does prepare others for the real world;
- To give all our children the same opportunity.

Fears about inclusion

- I will not be emotionally equipped to deal with these children;
- More less able children than able in any one school;
- Support being whittled away over time leading to extra burdens and stresses;
- Too much will be expected of us with too little support;
- Will it show that negative behaviour is OK?
- The mainstream children will not have access to the curriculum because of disruptive behaviour;
- Even more teachers will find alternative employment;
- Negative reaction from local community.

Solutions

- Bodies in classroom;
- Loads of money and commitment;
- A very gradual implementation of an inclusion policy;
- A hard-working, open-minded staff, with training;
- Units on-site;
- Efforts to diminish a culture of violence;
- Inclusion must be a societal thing – mixing areas, e.g. working-class people in middle-class areas;
- Resources matching children's needs;
- Education for parents;
- Making time to talk so staff don't feel lonely;
- Ban the phrase: 'My mum says, if someone hits me, hit them back.'

The project coordinator reflected on these responses and a number of issues emerged, for example: opinions vary from 'outright hostility to total acceptance', that people are anxious about resources, time and energy and that some schools are working towards inclusion but not disseminating their experiences. In her evaluation, the coordinator wrote:

> 'Special schools feel under pressure to find a mainstream school prepared to work alongside them, not the other way around. It is clear that a more equitable system for 'pairing' needs to be developed if this kind of imbalance is to be redressed. I have come

across only one instance of a mainstream school approaching a special school; interestingly, this has resulted in one of the most successful inclusion projects I have seen so far . . .

'Although attitudes of individual schools are an important factor in determining success, a piecemeal approach to inclusion is much less likely to be effective than a citywide strategy . . .

'When it comes down to the practicalities of "getting on" with planning for inclusion, all kinds of hurdles are put in the way by school staff. It is hard to pinpoint reasons for this resistance, but it is clear that many staff are reluctant to share information (give away power?) or to make anything other than very token changes to their working practices.

'There is a commonly held misconception that "special needs children" need very specialist and particular help and that school staff will be 'out of their depth". There is widespread misunderstanding about the kind of input and skills that will be needed and a belief that the teaching skills already possessed by staff have no relevance.

'There appears to be a hierarchy of inclusion, with children who have serious "emotional and behavioural difficulties" amongst the lowest on schools' priorities for inclusion.'

She concluded:

'The journey may be a gradual one – not everyone can move at the same pace – but the destination seems, to me, the only one to aim for if we are to live and work within systems that are just and fair.'

Chapter 4

Selection by attainment in Birmingham

Sharon Rustemier with Gwenn Edwards

INTRODUCTION

This chapter is about the processes by which young people attend comprehensive, grammar or special schools according to their educational achievements and perceived ability. After explaining how selection by attainment works in Birmingham, we introduce ourselves and the schools. We then make the case for including special and grammar schools within the same debate. Focusing on the views and experiences of staff and pupils at three schools we explore the effects of this selection by attainment on opportunities for educational inclusion in the city. We draw out for discussion the question of diversity at the level of the school or the system, the issues surrounding primary–secondary transfer, parental choice, and co-location as one response to the dilemmas raised.

HOW SELECTION BY ATTAINMENT WORKS IN BIRMINGHAM

There are 107 secondary schools in Birmingham (DfES 2001a). Of these fourteen are designated 'special' schools, seventy 'comprehensive', eight 'independent non-selective' and fifteen 'selective'. There are currently twenty-six schools with specialist status – fifteen in technology, five sports, four arts, and two languages – of which two are selective schools and seven are single-sex schools. All specialist schools are permitted to select up to 10 per cent of their intake.

Prior to a child's beginning secondary education, parents receive a booklet which provides information about the secondary schools available and the process by which parents express their preferences. It advises parents that choosing the nearest secondary school as a first preference is the best option, except 'if the school has previously filled at a closer distance than you live or applies special religious or other admission criteria'. It then warns, however, that distance will not be considered for those schools able to take all first-preference applicants. In schools maintained by the City Council, places are allocated first to children with statements of special educational need (SEN) 'in the case of certain schools with a designated unit which caters for them', although special schools per se are omitted from the booklet. After this, allocation is based on various combinations of factors involving siblings, distance and if the school is named as first, second or third preference.

Grammar schools require prospective students to sit selective tests (still referred to as 'the eleven-plus'), some administered by the County Council, others by the schools themselves. For admission in September 2002, the booklet lists eight grammar schools, giving figures for the number of places available and, as a guide, the number of applications made for places the previous year. For places in September 2001 there were 8,129 applications. The number of places available for 2002 is 991. Assuming that the intake figures remain fairly constant, this would predict somewhere in the region of 7,138 children beginning secondary education having 'failed' the eleven-plus selection process.

The chief education officer's introduction to the booklet suggests a certain similarity between schools:

> All secondary schools . . . have one shared purpose: each is determined to improve against its own previous best performance, which means that the staff are determined that each generation of pupils achieve ever higher standards. . . . [All] Birmingham schools . . . are part of the 'Excellence in Cities' programme which will mean substantial extra resources and opportunities for your child if they attend a Birmingham secondary school. In that sense you can feel confident that any of the city's schools will be a good choice: it is simply a matter of feeling confident that your youngster will be happy in the school he or she attends and that it suits his or her needs. . . . Those entering a secondary school in the year 2002 will in every sense be special.

However, as this chapter will show and as will be expected in a system which selects by attainment, some schools are more desirable than others, parity of esteem between different schools and types of schools is not a reality, and the decision can have life-determining consequences for the child.

INVESTIGATING SELECTION BY ATTAINMENT

In this chapter, we explore selection by attainment with reference to the systems, practitioners and pupils in three schools: a special school, a 'comprehensive' school, and a grammar school. We also talked to other teachers and students in the secondary sector. We draw on information gleaned from interviews, discussions, questionnaires, visits to schools, OFSTED reports, school prospectuses and league tables.

We approach the research from diverse perspectives, one of us as the 'insider', currently working as a teacher and mentor in a 'comprehensive' school in the city, the other as the 'outsider', committed to inclusive values derived from personal experience of comprehensive schooling, Oxbridge higher education and both segregated and community mental health provision, as well as involvement in similar research in another city.

The schools and people we worked with were chosen initially through professional contacts. However, while some readily agreed to be involved, 'insider' status did not help in relation to the grammar schools where access proved difficult. While we were able to engage grammar school pupils in the research, teachers were reluctant to speak with us 'on the record'. It was difficult to determine the reasons for this. Perhaps they saw themselves as somehow 'outside' the inclusion agenda, considered inclusion as irrelevant to them, were busy with admissions and selection exams at the time of the research, or there was some other reason.

THE SCHOOLS

In the north of the city, in a well-established residential area with several important areas of open space, the grammar is a girls' school with performing arts specialist status, serving 983 pupils aged from eleven to eighteen drawn from across the city. In 2001, 99 per cent of pupils achieved GCSE/GNVQ top grades, compared to a city average of 41 per cent and a national average of 50 per cent (DfES 2001a). Seven of the pupils (0.7 per cent) are considered to have special educational needs, though none has a statement; 4.1 per cent are eligible for free school meals.

The 'comprehensive' – a school with specialist technology status and a sixth form – is situated in a run-down neighbourhood but next to a thriving leisure and community centre in the central area of the city. In 2001 its intake was 1,248 pupils drawn from the immediate locality, including 10 per cent selected on apititude, 20.2 per cent with special educational needs but no statement, 0.9 per cent with statements, and 52.4 per cent eligible for free school meals. In 2001, 51 per cent of pupils achieved the top grades in GCSE/GNVQs, above the city and national averages.

The special school has 68 pupils aged from eleven to nineteen, all with statements of special educational need, and is described in its OFSTED report as a 'non-selective state special community school'. It stands in the central area of the city but south of the 'comprehensive', in a smart residential location. Its pupils come from all areas of the city, the majority from the south. None was entered for GCSE/GNVQs in 2001 and, as a special school, it is included on a separate list in the DfES performance tables (DfES 2001a).

It is omitted altogether from the *Guardian* tables 'in the interests of fairness' (Major 2001). The school shares performing arts college status with a nearby mainstream 'comprehensive' school, and there are plans to move to that school's site by 2003 ('co-location').

MAKING CONNECTIONS

It is not usual in research on inclusion or selection to discuss special schools and grammar schools in the same framework. The issues involving mainstream and special education, and comprehensive and grammar schools, are traditionally perceived and treated separately (e.g. see Edwards and Whitty 1997b; Montgomery and Gallagher 2000; DENI 2000; Crook *et al.* 1999). When attention is paid to the 'lower end' of the ability spectrum it tends to be in terms of secondary modern schools, not special schools (e.g. Walford 1994).

However, there are compelling reasons for making connections between special and grammar schools:

- The language of attainment and ability used to justify the 'creaming off' of the 'high achievers' from ordinary 'comprehensives' is part of that same discourse of disability and low achievement which is used to rationalize the segregation of the 'bottom' layer out of the mainstream – the language of difference and otherness applies to both;
- The effects of segregation by special school and by grammar school are the same: both represent the marginalization of certain young people from the main body of students, and make 'comprehensive' schools far from being comprehensive or schools for all;
- It is argued that both special schools and grammar schools meet students' particular needs in a way that purportedly cannot be achieved in mainstream 'comprehensive' schools, something further emphasized by the concept of 'specialist' secondary schools being promoted by government;
- Both play a crucial role in shaping students' future opportunities for educational and social inclusion;
- National government policy and legislation bypass the dilemmas thrown up by both forms of schooling by appealing to 'parental choice': thus grammar schools can exist so long as parents don't vote them out by ballot (School Standards and Framework Act 1998) and children can continue to be segregated in special schools so long as that is what parents wish (Special Educational Needs and Disability Act 2001); and
- Both reflect the government emphasis on exam achievements and standards, and belie the rhetoric about communities and inclusion.

VIEWS ON INCLUSION

Our discussion with members of staff in the schools reflected the wide range of views of inclusion held by educational professionals in Birmingham discussed in Chapter 2. The head teacher of the special school conceptualized inclusion in terms of rights and citizenship, and saw 'co-location' as the 'ideal' solution to the tensions between inclusion and selection on the grounds of disability and learning difficulty:

> 'Fundamentally I believe in equality and that includes inclusive practices. But by equality what I would refer to is every student in the context of education is entitled to the best education we can give them, but that is essentially not the same education for every person, and if they need support then they should get the support they require. Certainly, I believe in the breadth of educational opportunity. But I also believe in everybody's equal right to be a valued citizen, to take their place in society whatever their economic value to society is, and therefore I don't feel comfortable with special schools being isolated from mainstream schools. I see co-location as an ideal . . . because it means that we are embracing the best of potentials and setting a base from which education and a style of educational opportunity can evolve in a natural way not an enforced way. So what we're looking at is to have [the special school] intact but over the years to develop our own skills as teachers in both settings, to appreciate the job that each person does and in some instances be able to cross over that threshold so that we get a greater appreciation and ability to respond to a greater variety of needs.
>
> 'I think working with mainstream colleagues helps us to stay tuned in to what's current in schools. . . . [I]t's quite possible to lose sight of the fact that as our students go home to families they go into a mixed-ability environment. And it is normal for all of us to live in a mixed-ability, mixed-need, mixed-circumstance world, and we could deny our students a relationship with that world if we just keep the doors closed and say that we do what we do very nicely thank you, leave us alone. I think there's a much greater responsibility and onus upon us to look to the whole person, and the whole person is the person within the community, which starts with the family.
>
> 'So, as I say, in moving I think that working with mainstream colleagues and with mainstream peers for our students, it keeps afresh the knowledge of where we are as a community. I think we learn so much over time. We learn how the mainstream student will relate to our students, and the effect that that has on our students, and that is basically what it can teach us, it can teach us new ways to do things. It certainly continues to motivate us along the pathway that we've embarked upon towards maximum inclusive practice but whilst protecting the best interests of our students.'

So what she called co-location was actually about much more than where learning takes place. She went on to discuss the importance of relationships and attitudes, and the interaction between people from the mainstream and others:

'It's very easy for the adults to make assumptions and adults, in making assumptions, can make a prophecy a reality. And I think that many of us are restricted in our beliefs towards inclusive practice because of our own history. . . . [W]e're the people that shape things and . . . we can make things work or we can sabotage things with our own fears or assumptions. So when [mainstream] students come in and we observe how they interact they're not bringing prejudices of history that maybe we would assume they would have – so it stops us making assumptions.'

Student council members, with the aid of photographs and a communications facilitator, also referred to working and learning together when speaking of co-location. One pupil, Karen, had brought to our meeting a list of concerns about co-location compiled by her classmates which centred on social and organizational matters:

Will the people be nice?

Will we have friends there?

Will there be help to find our way there on the bus?

How will we find our way round the building?

Can we take our bags and coats into the school?

Will our break times be the same?

Will the journey to school be long?

However, there was also a great deal of emphasis – mainly through the facilitator's promptings – on the resource benefits of moving to the mainstream site. For example:

David: I did drama with [the mainstream school] students. It was good to have a partner to work with. The rooms [there] are big. They have a special music room. . . .
Facilitator: That's what you like about [that] school, isn't it, that they've got special rooms for special lessons. I think that's what we all like.
Kate: How many rooms will there be?
Facilitator: How many rooms do we have here?
Kate: Not many.

Facilitator: And what happens to our rooms? Do we go to the art room to do art? Do we go to the cookery room to do cookery? Do we go to the music room to do music?

Sian: No we have to bring the stuff to our class.

Facilitator: You're right, we have to bring everything to the room we're in. We bring the cooker, we bring the music, we bring the art. Wouldn't it be good to have special rooms for special lessons?

In informal discussion following the meeting, the facilitator highlighted the importance of the special school students 'retaining their own identity' and again stressed the long-established need for better resources, explaining that the inadequacy of current accommodation was because the school had originally been a primary school.

The special school staff's confidence in talking about inclusion may result from the City Council's historical focus on inclusion as an SEN issue (see Chapter 2). Other practitioners interviewed seemed on less certain ground when discussing inclusion, or saw inclusion only in terms of reducing disciplinary exclusion. For example, the head of learning support at the 'comprehensive' stated that 'we [the school] do have some very firm views on inclusion,' but when asked about these in relation to our conversation about faith, gender and attainment divisions in and between schools, the comprehensiveness of the intake of 'comprehensive' schools, and collaboration between schools, she related the concept only to disciplinary exclusions:

> 'Well, at this school we have what's called the learning support base. . . . [Our] programme has been hailed as good practice for the rest of the city. . . . We don't put children in isolation for a four-week period, in a base, where they don't see any teachers. Our aim is to get those children fully back into mainstream curriculum as quickly as possible. . . . There may be some lessons where they are withdrawn for a while and go to the base with support to work on the programme of work that they would be doing. So we don't have children excluded for a bulk period of time. And it works very well. And [we] do a lot of work with the staff. I think that's important, too, it's not just withdrawing children and then putting them back in, it's the INSET with the staff and the advice and support those staff get that makes it successful here. . . . I don't think we have excluded anyone long-term for about four years now. Short-term exclusions, yes – a week, maybe. And even those aren't very common.

> 'And I think it's a lot to do with the ethos of the school that's built up over the years. I mean the previous head called this school his family and that's continued, and when children come here the message is put out that you are part of this family. And it does make a difference to a lot of the children. And, yes, we have our difficult kids – I mean, every school

does – and the base, you see, is open to the children at lunchtimes and breaktimes so they can go at any time they feel they want to just talk to somebody and say look I feel that I'm not getting on particularly well with such-and-such a subject, can you help me? And they'll go and work with the teacher again and it's very good.'

However, alongside this positive attitude to working with pupils under threat of exclusion within the school was a relief that, as an oversubscribed school, it was under no pressure to include children excluded from other schools:

'We're quite fortunate in that situation. I've also been in a school where they weren't oversubscribed and you end up having to take in other children, so we don't at the moment take in other children which have been excluded from other schools.'

This willingness to work with children at risk of exclusion but reluctance to accept those already excluded indicates the finality of the act of exclusion in a child's life. Similarly, the head teacher of the special school noted the finality of segregation into special school at the primary–secondary transfer:

'By the time the students have reached eleven the divide between the mainstream and [special] secondary is vast compared with primary . . . and as we're taking the students in at eleven, people will have made those decisions through debates that don't reach us. So [transfer to mainstream secondary schooling is] not likely to happen, but that's where we would hope the opportunities to be placed alongside mainstream would come into their own.'

IMPACT ON NON-SELECTIVE SCHOOLS

We asked practitioners about the effects of selective schools on the pupil intake of other schools. The non-pressure on oversubscribed schools – and over half the secondary schools in the city are oversubscribed – to accept excluded pupils clearly means these children are concentrated in the other undersubscribed schools, arguably perpetuating the differential desirability of schools underpinning parental choice. The head of learning support at the 'comprehensive' also made the link between better resourcing, oversubscription and achievement:

'The school was one of the first schools to become grant maintained in Birmingham, and of course at the time the GM schools had a lot of extra money and were able to control their own finances so that helped. And then it became a technology college, I think in '96, so again it was one of the earlier specialist schools, and I think it has just gradually evolved . . . and exam results have gone up dramatically over the last few years. It's a very popular school in the area.'

The 'comprehensiveness' of non-selective schools is also affected by selective schools in terms of gender, ethnic diversity and faith. After speaking of the possible effect of a proposed nearby faith school which is likely to attract female students from the area, the head of learning support drew attention to the comprehensive's own ethnically skewed intake:

'Our intake is interesting as well because it's 98 per cent Muslim, and although we insist that we are not a faith school I sometimes wonder whether the local perception is that we are because of the large intake. And we would like to encourage more children from other backgrounds to come, but again that's difficult because parents, much as they rate the school, have to weigh up considerations as well as to the social life of the children. In our current Year 11 we've got one pupil who's not a Muslim, and her parents want her to come here because they perceive it's a school that gets good exam results, but she is very isolated and doesn't have a real best friend and that's a real problem.'

In contrast, discussion with practitioners in the special school revealed a perception of gender and ethnicity as virtually a 'non-issue' in terms of the diversity among pupils, reinforcing the perceived 'otherness' of these young people. The deputy head teacher answered my question about the ethnicity of pupils in the school: 'I'd guess, a very rough guess, 20 per cent students of Asian origin – now obviously that's the range of ethnic groups there. Quite a small number from the Caribbean origin. And the rest are basically white UK.' On the question of gender, he simply stated: 'Genetic disorders are just much more prevalent in boys.'

SPECIALIST STATUS

Since all three schools in our study had specialist status, and since the government sees such status as a means to both benefit parental choice and increase diversity within the education system, we were interested in the impact of this status on these and other schools.

Practitioners in the special school saw the specialist status as recognition of their long-established success in the performing arts and, most importantly, as providing the resources and impetus for pursuing co-location with their partner mainstream school. The head teacher explained:

'It took a long time to find a partner to work with in the first place that was receptive to the notion of working very closely together and to cementing the partnership but also in a position to be able to receive another school. There were people I spoke to who were interested from the philosophical side in working together, but in practical terms it was a non-starter because their site couldn't accommodate our students. But the arts have formed, I think, quite a significant link of understanding. We're talking about two schools that value the arts and see them as a means of breaking down barriers and giving opportunities to students who are challenged in other ways and that was as equal a truth from their mainstream perspective as ours. And [we have] had a very strong reputation in the arts, so we weren't going into the discussions as weak partners and were seen as, I think, being worthy staff-wise to have exchanged, not only in the arts but to learn from each other. . . .

'It was certainly seen as an opening tool for the two schools to find some common platform . . . we'd behaved as a specialist school for the arts for a long time now, but we're more motivated towards the partnership for co-location than gaining specialist college status. . . . [T]hose partnerships are constantly developing because through the jointness we have to keep talking together, we have to make the effort to work together, so that sustains us even through more difficult times, with staff changes and anything like that. I think it's a unity that will continue to be important.'

The deputy head teacher added:

'In terms of what I call real resourcing it has made a huge difference. Links between special and mainstream have always happened but now it happens on a much more systematic basis . . . now we can actually plan it into the curriculum.'

In addition to allowing the school to select 10 per cent of its intake on aptitude in technology, though still from the local area, specialist status at the 'comprehensive' contributed significantly to its outreach work with local primary schools:

'I think the days have gone when we all sort of work behind closed doors and say, 'Well, we're not going to help you because you might pinch our ideas.' . . . And, being a specialist technology college, we have a community plan – all specialist schools have to have a community plan as well as a school plan – and that is to work more with secondary schools and primary schools, and we do a lot with the local primary schools. They love coming in and bringing their classes here, using the technology, doing science, doing maths.

'Not so easy with the secondary schools really. . . . I think timetabling issues are more difficult – aren't they? – with secondary schools. I think maybe there is a sort of sentimental reluctance, you know: "Well, what's in it for us? What will we get out of it?" And it always has been easier to work with feeder primary schools because you have that inbuilt link anyway – we know that we'll get most of those Year 6 children through Year 7 so the Year 6 teacher will bring them in and they'll teach technology with them and they'll walk back to their school and that's easy to set up and arrange, whereas for secondary schools you might phone up and say "Would you like to bring yours in for technology lessons?", they might argue when and why, and "That doesn't coincide with our technology lessons, our facilities are OK, thank you very much." So you're having to break down barriers there.'

The head teacher of the special school was less positive about the impact of specialist status on community outreach work:

'Oh, it is generally known that that is the weakest side and I think there's good reason for that because a third of your budget has to be spent on community ventures, but if you think of extending into the community from an already fairly exhausted resource, you're talking about having to significantly staff over and above what you were staffing before you became an arts college, and on this we're only 50 per cent of an arts college because we're two schools. But I think we're probably expected to do as much as two individual arts colleges but on a smaller budget. So we have to keep reminding people about the restrictions.'

PARENTAL CHOICE

While the primary–secondary transition is the principal site for the operation of selection by attainment, parental choice is considered to be a major factor in the process. Most – though not all – pupils participating in our work felt that they too had had at least some involvement in this decision-making. One teacher at the 'comprehensive' turned during our discussion to her own dilemmas in choosing a school for her son:

'It's very very difficult to find in some areas what you could call a true comprehensive school with a true comprehensive intake, and the grammar schools affect that. . . .

'My son had the option of sitting the eleven-plus and he didn't want to, so we thought: fine. And we were basically left with a very limited choice.

The schools that I've mentioned, [one] he couldn't go to because we're not Catholic. . . . He didn't want to go [to a single-sex school]. So it's [the other comprehensive] that we've got his name down for, and I'm not entirely happy, and one of the reasons I'm not entirely happy is the exam results are not particularly good, so that's obviously a parental concern, and out of five forms in Year 7 only two of those are mixed. The other three are all-boy forms, again because of the girls schools. . . . The things in its favour were that it's within spitting distance of where we live and it's a small school. . . . I think a small school can make for a more settled transition from primary school. . . . So that's it really, we'll have to keep our fingers crossed and hope that he survives it all right. I think it's as comprehensive as they come in the area because there's quite a rough lower end but quite a good top end as well. . . . The other reason that we did put [that school] is that his best friend is going there and they wanted to go together.'

She went on to comment:

'It's all very well to say that, well, parents can choose to send their child to any school, but you can't in practice because schools have limited numbers. I can't here take in a child that lives over in Kings Heath because we have to have siblings and those nearest to the school, and that fills the school up. I mean, we could fill the school twofold with people living in this area.'

As noted above, however, while the intake at the 'comprehensive' school was primarily from the local area, pupils at the grammar and special schools came from across the city. More than half the twenty-three grammar school pupils who gave us their views routinely travelled for more than thirty minutes to get to school, many for over an hour. This mobility issue is an important factor in parental choice, the more affluent households with the means of transporting their children long distances to school if not actually of moving nearer the school, having an advantage over the less affluent and less mobile households.

However, this mobility can have a less positive effect on the pupils. The journeys themselves can be burdensome. One boy that we interviewed who had withdrawn from his grammar school twice referred to the burden of the long journeys to and from school in talking about the 'pressures' he had experienced during his time there. Travelling across the city to school also severely limits opportunities for forming friendships in local neighbourhoods. Rather, grammar-school pupils form friendships with other high attainers while pupils at special school have little opportunity to form relationships with non-disabled young people. Issues of mobility are discussed further in Chapter 8.

We spoke to another comprehensive school teacher, who had decided to send his son to a grammar school. He explained:

'I think it would be a lot easier to make the decision about supporting a local secondary school if it was a girl. It is difficult when you work in schools . . . even though I'm perceived to be knowledgeable in education, my experience of other schools is limited, and I'm not necessarily convinced that I have an accurate idea of what my son's experience will be like. . . .

'I suppose what I've learned over my time raising children – which goes back to the mid 70s – is that I've become much more flexible. I don't rule things out in advance maybe as I used to, and I would certainly consider looking at that [grammar] option . . . I would actually consider the option, believe it or not, of paying, if I had the money. I suppose I've come to the conclusion that . . . you have one opportunity. I mean, obviously, there are chances later in life but those critical years between eleven and eighteen, essentially you have one go at it and a lot depends on it, or at least that's how it feels, so I don't sort of rule things out like I used to. . . . Part of this has to do with the kind of person I think that I perceive my son to be. I mean, we talked the other day about how well equipped a child might be at the age of eleven to cope with the hurly-burly of a school like [where I teach]. . . . But, yes, it partly has to do with the make-up of the child, psychological make-up if you like, how vulnerable I might perceive him to be. I guess all parents perceive their children to be vulnerable, I mean that's part of what being a parent's all about.'

He went on to talk about the possibility that his son might fail the selection exam:

'That is a very real consideration. Otherwise you're always talking about what if, and how will we ensure that the damage, if there is going to be damage, is minimized. We'd want to be relatively confident, as I think a lot of parents would feel the same way, they want to be relatively confident that their son would do well enough, not suffer from the experience. In some ways that's an argument for putting him in for everything because they get more opportunities. . . . I find myself in this strange kind of situation of thinking, because my [older] son's experience of going to a public school was so much better in terms of the freedom, creativity, the relationships between the teachers and the students, the opportunities he had to do things outside of the classroom, the sporting opportunities, he did a lot of drama, he did a lot of creative arts stuff. . . . But . . . wouldn't we want that for everybody?

'But when you're at that point of making the choice, you're not choosing for everybody. That belongs to a different area of your life, maybe some political activism or some debate that's going on. At the point when you're making the choice it's about your own child . . . I'm not making the choice for everybody . . . I'm involved in making it for him. . . . It's about trying to be flexible and open to what I perceive to be, however limited my understanding, however limited my bank balance, the range of choices that are available to us. It would be a nice decision not to have to make.'

When asked about parental choice at the special school, the deputy head teacher explained what he called 'the transition process':

'We go out and, well, all parents are encouraged to visit as part of the city-wide process of choosing their child's secondary school so parents visit at that stage. Then as part of the transition process our Year 7 teacher is very experienced in that role and will go out and meet those pupils in the schools, take questionnaires and talk to staff who we've got to know very well over the years anyway. Then those children visit with support from their schools for a morning and then visit for a morning together with support from our staff. On that same morning all other pupils in the school go to their next class for the morning, to the staff they will be with in September, so that process is planned quite carefully. We always hold a parents' evening in October as well as the annual review which tends to be in the summer because it's just as important for staff to meet pupils early in the school year as later because otherwise you have the frustration of 'Oh well, if I'd have known that. . . .''

STUDENTS' VIEWS

We asked a group of students in a 'comprehensive' school about their primary–secondary transitions. Some had taken and failed the eleven-plus exam; others had opted directly for the 'comprehensive' school. Their comments revealed their perceptions of grammar schools. For example, when asked had they thought about going to a grammar school and why, one answered, 'Yes, because I thought that no other schools can achieve such education.' Others said:

'Yes, because the standard of learning in grammar schools is better than in ordinary schools.'

'Yes because you'll have a better education and school life would probably be a lot easier.'

'I did think about going to a grammar school while I was in primary school because that was the best education available and I wanted that.'

'Yes, I did because I heard they were schools that really tested you and they had better levels and grades.'

'Yes, I wanted to go to one because I thought I would get a better education.'

'No, because you have to be quite clever to get in and I wasn't clever.'

'Yes, because there you don't waste time and you are always challenged a bit more.'

'No, this is because I didn't want to be in a school where if I was a little less bright than someone else I would be feeling dumb.'

This perception of higher standards at the grammar school was reinforced by the views of the majority of the pupils from the grammar school, who referred to the 'better standards' and 'better education' to be gained there. One said: 'I chose to go to a grammar school because I didn't want to go to the comprehensive schools in my area because of the lower standards and expectations.' Some linked this with better long-term opportunities and getting a 'good start in life'.

Other perceptions of grammar school were revealed when pupils were asked directly about their opinions of the selective system. Many associated grammar schools with single-sex and/or fee-paying schools, clearly perceiving them in terms of privilege as well as ability. For example:

'I think that grammar schools work better than normal mixed-sex schools. I think this because if there is only single-sex then classes will be smaller so it is easier to focus on teaching students.'

'I don't think that people should take exams or pay to go to secondary school as it makes people think they are the best if they can afford to pay for education.'

'I think selective schools is just a way of getting extra money for the school.'

'Selective schools – I don't think there's much point. Why pay when you can get it free?'

Others commented on the inequalities and separations inherent in the system:

'I think schools such as grammar are very good due to the high level of education and exam results. But are quite unfair because kids with the exam marks they look for are allowed to enter. But I think everyone has the potential to do well and kids not getting [in] may be put down thinking they're not capable.'

'I am not very keen on selective schools. I think that all children should have equal opportunities. You shouldn't get a better standard of education simply because you are clever. Everyone deserves to [be] treated the same regardless of whether they are as capable as some.'

'I think grammar schools are unnecessary. How can a school give you better education just because of an exam? I think all schools should have the same standard of education.'

'Grammar schools are good but I don't like how it separates you from other students. It makes me feel that they are superior to me.'

'I didn't think they were a good idea as going to a grammar school meant you couldn't mix with people on different levels, everyone would be the same.'

When asked how they perceived the education they had received, the comprehensive school pupils who had 'failed' their eleven-plus exam gave similar comments to those who had gone straight for the 'comprehensive' in the first place, i.e. mostly positive but with some difficulties with teachers. For example:

'The education I've had has been very successful, helping me achieve good results and improving year by year. I think it is at a good standard.'

'I think the education has [been] fairly good. Some teachers can't teach but [the] majority of the teaching is very good.'

'It is great because we've had many good teachers over the bad ones. Also, it is not just education, it is humour.'

'I think the education I have had has been fairly good: eight out of ten. A lot of assets. Teachers have left, which, I personally think, has dropped the standards a little.'

'I think the education I've had is quite good so far, but it affects me when I have [a] supply teacher or when I have to change teachers after being taught from them for so long.'

'I think the education is quite good here. I think I can achieve good grades because the teachers do a brilliant job at teaching.'

On the other hand, pupils at the grammar school were generally more satisfied. They referred far more frequently to the 'high standard' of education they felt they were receiving, although some were also critical of 'poor' teaching and 'too big' classes. One felt her education had a 'judgemental tinge to it'; another: 'It's good. But being as I have never attended a comprehensive school, I can't compare it.'

A young man we spoke to who had attended another grammar school had been particularly unhappy with his experiences:

'There was a lot of pressure to do as well as you could and to do all the work on time and I think those were the main problems . . . combined with the travelling and the way they made you feel, like you were given this gift to go to this school so you had to do well at all costs which I think in the end turned me against the school and worked against me . . . just the whole ambience of "You're here because you've earned your place, and there's thousands of people that would kill to be in your position", which made it very hard to concentrate when the going got tough. The work wasn't easy either; you were pushed very hard. I think it's very institutionalized so if you don't fit the bill it's hard . . . because people were, like, telling you all the time that you're privileged to be here so you must do this and you must do that. . . .

'I think, looking back, it was kind of like it was a decision made by my mum really. She wanted the best for me. I felt that if I'd known what I know now then obviously it would have been different. . . . I think that I missed a lot of the things that you could never learn by going to a school like that, just the getting on with other people, different cultures, and the local experience. . . . I did make a lot of friends from a lot of different areas. I suppose that was the thing, everyone had to come so far so you made friends, but it means you didn't know anyone in your home area. I had one friend who lived [near my home] but that was it.'

As already mentioned, the special school students focused on co-location, reported above.

DISCUSSION

So, what can all this tell us about inclusion and selection by attainment? How can inclusion work in a system which continues to select and segregate pupils according to attainment?

The government answer is to focus on the level of the education system rather than the individual school. The coexistence of grammar and comprehensive schools has been a feature of many LEAs, and systemic diversity continues to be fostered (Crook *et al.* 1999). However, the system in Birmingham clearly demonstrates that for every school that selects its pupils, opportunities for inclusion are lost and comprehensive schooling for other pupils ceases to be an option. Diversity between rather than within schools is also the argument frequently underpinning those who emphasize the 'needs met' factor (see Walford 1994): there are particularly 'bright' students and particularly disabled students whose needs cannot be met in an ordinary state secondary school, necessitating the existence of grammar and special schools.

This argument reflects a very narrow conception of the process and purpose of education, and the consequent separation of groups of young people impoverishes rather than enriches their educational experience. Far from encouraging the development of socially competent individuals and an inclusive society, grouping according to exam results creates supposedly homogeneous groups based on achievement and reinforces social divisions, denying young people the experience of variety and diversity offered by a more inclusive approach.

The primary–secondary transfer is the chief site at which decisions are made that have lifelong consequences. However, the idea that there is a fixed point in a child's life where a decision has irreversible consequences is, of course, one of the major arguments against the eleven-plus exam. It is also at odds with the idea of promoting inclusion and involving young people in decisions which affect them. By severely curtailing their options from this point, it also denies them one of the most fundamental aspects of humanity: the capacity for self-determination. From this point, the differences between pupils become institutionalized and formalized. The consequences of this division mean that many children's lives are systematically impoverished, and that 'successes' are more the exception than the rule, achievement despite rather than because of the system (see Chapter 7).

Another problem with this systemic diversity argument is that it assumes parity of esteem between different schools and types of schools and a level playing field among parents choosing where to send their children for their secondary education. In fact, this chapter has shown clearly that not all schools are held in equal regard. Grammar schools are perceived in terms of privilege, providing a better standard of education and superior resources. The entry criteria for special schools include having a statement of SEN and disabilities or difficulties in learning that cannot be catered for in the mainstream. Even within the comprehensive sector, specialist status, league tables and oversubscription have created a hierarchy of desirability. Moreover, the operation of a selective system militates against some options altogether. The evidence is that so long as schools select, the option of a truly comprehensive or inclusive school does not exist. The secondary school system may be diverse, but its members are not equally valued. It is not inclusive.

We should also question whether parental choice – what the chief education officer called inclusion's 'biggest virus' (see Chapter 2) – really has the significance accorded it. Parents can choose the eleven-plus but have no control over whether or not their children pass. If their child has a statement of SEN they can choose segregated provision, but even under the recent Special Educational Needs and Disability Act 2001 their choice of mainstream school would be constrained by a number of conditions. In fact, it is often the schools selecting the pupils rather than parents choosing the schools (and see Edwards and Whitty, 1997a). The idea that different schools having different focii and characteristics (specialization) encourages parental choice and is not the same as selection, where the schools do the choosing, can be traced back to the Conservative government of the early 1990s (DfEE, 1992). However, this chapter has demonstrated that such specialization, or systemic diversity, actually reduces parental choice precisely because it is selective (and see Edwards and Whitty, 1997b).

Where parents do choose, however, this in itself is problematic. The separation of the personal and political used to justify one comprehensive school teacher's decision to send his son to grammar school and described in this chapter can be challenged since every choice has a social impact. Moreover, to argue that parents can choose selection is a denial of inclusiveness.

Parental choice means that the diversity between schools fosters competition and works against the collaboration that would characterize inclusive practice. Although many initiatives are aimed at developing collaborative working between schools – including 'excellence' clusters, Beacon schools, specialist status – this rarely happens in practice (see Chapter 8, and OFSTED, 2001). Schools continue to view themselves as individuals and in competition with one another for students and resources.

The notion of co-location – one response to the challenge of inclusion being pursued in the city – throws up further significant issues. It moves towards collaborative working which in itself might indicate inclusive practice; it apparently solves the problem of competition for resources; and it involves students from segregated groups working together and at least beginning to form relationships. However, it also harbours tensions and contradictions.

One of the main difficulties with co-location is that it does not involve rethinking the mainstream and therefore does little to challenge the divisions institutionalized by the selection by attainment in the first place. Despite their attention to opportunities for forming new relationships and ways of working, the emphasis by the special school practitioners on retaining the school's identity and 'protecting' the interests of the students perpetuates the fundamental perception of otherness underpinning the initial segregation of mainstream and special school students. The idea of working together but maintaining a separate identity does nothing to address the root causes of difference and stereotypical thinking which characterize the selective system.

Similarly, although in terms of resources the special school students will undoubtedly be better off as a result of the co-location project discussed in this chapter, again this does not challenge the inequalities inherent in the system. The issue of resources is commonly cited against the inclusion of students with disabilities in mainstream education. On the other hand, it is also frequently used by the government as a rationale behind various initiatives to promote collaboration to break down barriers in education, as in the recent announcement of funding for links between private and state schools (BBC News Online, 21 November 2001). Of course, resources are important. However, when collaboration is based on sharing facilities and resources rather than on a fundamental reconceptualization of relationships between hitherto segregated groups, inclusion is an illusion and inequalities remain unaddressed. Sharing resources without reconceptualizing the relationships of all involved does little to address inequalities of power and privilege.

CONCLUSION

We set out to explore how the system of selection by attainment in Birmingham secondary schools impacted on opportunities for educational inclusion in the city. Through considering the cases of schools representing the whole spectrum of attainment we have highlighted a number of issues which cut to the heart of New Labour's approach to education. The existence of special and grammar schools has far-reaching consequences for young people in terms of their educational and social experiences and opportunities. It is less about parental choice than about adherence to a tangle of assumptions concerning inherent ability/disability and privilege. Inclusion and selection by attainment are incompatible because the outcome of selection by attainment is a collection of groups of young people segregated from one another.

However, this does not mean that attainment and inclusion are incompatible. The problem lies with the assumption that raising standards must mean separating those who perform at different levels of achievement, an assumption underpinning much government policy. The acknowledgement tucked away in the statutory guidance on the new framework for inclusion (DfES 2001b) that schools which have systematically attempted to develop inclusive practices have actually seen standards rise will remain at the level of impotent rhetoric unless it is accompanied by the political will to address those taboo areas of parental choice and the very existence of special and grammar schools.

REFERENCES

BBC *News Online*, 21 November 2001, 'State and Private Partnerships Funded', 21-11-01, 00:21, news.bbc.co.uk

BCC (2001) *Secondary Education Opportunities for Your Child in Birmingham 2002*, Birmingham: City Council Education Service.

Crook, D., Power, S. and Whitty, G. (1999) *The Grammar School Question: A Review of Research on Comprehensive and Selective Education*, London: Institute of Education.

DENI (2000) 'The Effects of the Selective System of Secondary Education in Northern Ireland', *Research Briefing* RB4/2000, Bangor, NI: Department of Education for Northern Ireland.

DfEE (1992) *Choice and Diversity: A New Framework for Schools*, London: HMSO.

DfES (2001a) *Birmingham Secondary School Performance Tables November 2001*, London: DfES Publications.

DfES (2001b) *Inclusive Schooling – Children with Special Educational Needs*, London: DfES Publications.

Edwards, T. and Whitty, G. (1997a) 'Marketing Quality: Traditional and Modern Versions of Academic Excellence', in Glatter, R. *et al.* (eds) (1997), 29–43.

Edwards, T. and Whitty, G. (1997b) 'Specialisation and Selection in Secondary Education', *Oxford Review of Education* 23 (1): 5–15.

Glatter, R., Woods, P.A. and Bagley, C. (eds) (1997) *Choice and Diversity in Schooling: Perspectives and Prospects*, London: Routledge.

Major, L.E. (2001) 'About the Tables' (*Guardian*, 20 November 2001).

Montgomery, A-M. and Gallagher, T. (2000) 'Survery of Selective Schools in England', selection project ref. SEL9.3, Bangor, NI: Department of Education for Northern Ireland.

OFSTED (2001) *Specialist Schools: An Evaluation of Progress*, London: OFSTED.

Walford, G. (1994) 'A Return to Selection?', *Westminster Studies in Education* 17: 19–30.

Chapter 5

Embracing the faith, including the community?

Tony Booth

In this chapter I look at selection by religion, and the effects this has on the relationship between schools and their communities. The study focuses in turn on a Catholic, an Anglican and an Islamic school and on representatives of their respective education coordinating bodies. I discuss selection criteria and how these are modified when the composition of neighbourhoods change. I look at the demand for Islamic schools and the reactions to their state funding. The chapter presents snapshots of practice and opinion. These change, but their implications for policy, and their contribution to an understanding of inclusion/exclusion, endure.

WHY STUDY SELECTION BY RELIGION?

Any detailed attempt to understand the development of inclusive, or comprehensive community education, has to engage with faith schools, though this has been neglected. State education in England grew out of a system based on denomination schools, dominated by the Church of England. About 20 per cent of schools are affiliated to the Church of England and about 10 per cent are Catholic (Chadwick 1997). There are about twenty-five state-funded Jewish schools, two state-funded Islamic primary schools, a voluntary-aided Islamic secondary school and a Sikh school. The private sector contains many additional, usually small, religious foundation schools including over sixty Islamic schools. The denomination of a school affects who from the surrounding communities is welcomed into membership of that school, and how staff and student members, of and not of the faith, participate within it.

There are pressures to increase the numbers of faith schools. The Dearing review of Anglican involvement in education recommended the establishment of a hundred new Anglican secondary schools (Archbishops' Council 2000). Many Muslims are keen to increase the number of Islamic schools. A debate about whether Islamic schools should qualify for the same state funding as Christian schools has been waged in previous years (Halstead 1988, National

Union of Teachers 1984), though more recently there has been an official acknowledgement that people of all faiths should have the same rights to establish and gain funding for their schools. An increase in faith schools is supported by government through the Education Bill working its way through Parliament in 2002.

Church leaders have been concerned to demonstrate that faith schools can also be 'inclusive'. The outgoing Archbishop of Canterbury called for faith schools to be 'inclusive' of people of other faiths and of no faith (*Times Education Supplement* 11 January 2002, p.17). The Archbishop of Birmingham, head of the Roman Catholic education service in England and Wales, defended the increased funding for faith schools, arguing that no school is 'truly inclusive at the point of entry. But all should be "inclusive" in the wider and wiser sense of educating people for active participation in an inclusive society.' (*Times Education Supplement* 11 January 2002, p.8). However, others have expressed strong opposition. Frank Dobson, Member of Parliament and ex-Minister, sees the increasing separation of children by faith as contributing to a 'ghastly society' in which groups are 'at each other's throats' (BBC Radio 4 *The Week in Westminster*, 9 February 2002). Concern about the increase in faith schools came in the wake of the 2001 riots in northern cities, following National Front activity. These had drawn attention to the disaffection of some young Muslims as well as to ethnic divisions between communities. Faith schools in these cities played a part in exacerbating and cementing such divisions (Home Office 2001). Such reactions were strengthened after the alleged involvement of people claiming allegiance to Islam in the loss of life at the World Trade Centre on 11 September 2001, which led to war in Afghanistan and raised feelings about hierarchies of faith and death. Frank Dobson proposed an amendment to the Education Bill – that faith schools should have to offer at least 25 per cent of their places to children not of the designated faith – but this was defeated.

In Northern Ireland, the persistence of religious denomination schools has long interacted with the ethnic and sectarian divisions, and has been seen by many as a barrier to lasting peace (Murray, Smith and Birthistle 1997). The issue was highlighted in the world media by coverage of violent demonstrations attempting to prevent Catholic children from walking to their school through a Protestant area (Bunting 2001). In that province, 'integration' is used to mean Catholics and Protestants being taught in the same schools with instruction being given in both the Catholic and Protestant religions (McLenahan, Cairns, Dunn and Morgan 1993). In fact, the first 'integrated schools' in Northern Ireland were special schools although this point is missing from most discussions of the issue. It is as if categorization as 'disabled' or 'having special needs' replaces all other aspects of a person's identity. The first integrated non-special school in Northern Ireland was a private school, Langan College, which opened in 1981 and only achieved full state funding in 1990 (Chadwick 1994).

Catholic schools began to be established in the first half of the nineteenth century during a period of increasing Irish migration to England. According to Mary Hickman it emerged because of objections from other denominations, in particular the Church of England but also the Conservative Party, to 'allow(ing) children of Irish Catholic migrants being schooled with other working-class children' (Hickman 1995: 155). Such histories are critically relevant to an understanding of present attitudes. I encountered a parallel story of the development of Muslim education in response to a sense of exclusion within state schools both in Birmingham and in other cities.

At the time of the study there were ten Catholic secondary schools, who have formed themselves into 'a Catholic partnership' and fifty-six primary schools. In contrast there were fifty-three Church of England primary schools but only one secondary school remaining from three. Thirty-six per cent of primary and 14 per cent of secondary schools were denominational. The Islamic school was one of the first two Islamic schools in England to attract state funding. The allocation of state funding to this Muslim school sharpened the arguments within the city about the desirability of religion-based schools.

INTRODUCING THE SCHOOLS

The voluntary-aided Anglican secondary school (School A) is on the edge of the inner city. It was the only remaining Church of England secondary school in the city, and the head teacher attached herself to the Catholic partnership of secondary schools. It had been one of three, but the other two, both in the inner city, had not adapted to changes in neighbourhood. It was built in the 1960s next to the dominating nineteenth-century Church of St ———. The church is described by the head of religious education as 'very high church ... it's more Catholic than the Catholics'. There are strong links wth the Catholic, Baptist and United Reform Churches. The school is 200 metres from the Central Mosque. Over 50 per cent of the school population were from families with a Muslim background. It had 350 students who between them spoke twenty-three home languages.

The Catholic primary school (School C), of about 200 students, is on the outskirts of the city in a mixed area economically but a predominantly white neighbourhood. It, too, is voluntary aided. The religious order attached to the school preserved the conservative traditions of the Catholic Church; mass was said in Latin and the priest faced the altar with his back to the congregation. The school building was modern open-plan, which the head teacher thought of as 'almost a contradiction' with the conservative views of the priests. The conservatism of the worshippers at the church meant that many of the parents were not attracted to the services. The head teacher would have liked there to be a family mass on Sundays but 'they are not prepared to upset those who come for the Latin mass. Change is very slow.'

The Islamic primary school (School I) emerged from a study group, established in 1989 to support parents who were educating their secondary-age daughters at home because they were not prepared to send them to mixed-sex schools. It eventually incorporated a mixed primary department which eventually received government funding. The new school took 210 pupils and had a waiting list of 1,500. The school provided a curriculum which respected religious concerns but also met the requirements of the national curriculum. Most of the students spoke one of six home languages: Malay, Urdu, Arabic Bengali, Gujerati and English. This last group, who had at least one parent whose first language was English, made up about 40 per cent of the pupils and included 'Afro-Caribbean, children of mixed heritage and three Asian-Pakistani origin families'.

SERVING THE FAITHFUL OR SERVING THE NEIGHBOURHOOD?

To what extent should religious denomination schools select students on the basis of religion? To what extent should they serve their surrounding communities? Such questions posed dilemmas for both the Catholic and Anglican Churches. As expressed by the Church of England diocesan director of education:

> 'Within any of our schools we would want to provide opportunities for the development of the Church of England faith. This is not indoc-trination, shoving it down someone's throat but within a Church of England school there should be an opportunity for any pupil to grow in Christian faith if they so wish.
>
> 'We have a *dilemma* in the Church of England because our trustees talk about schools for the *local* community . . . we would hope that the parishes and schools would be welcoming to all faiths and have a role as the *established* faith to help bind communities together. If we fear anything we fear segregation of communities which could happen.'

In addition to a wish to reach out to others of different faiths (though not explicitly those whose spirituality is not expressed in a particular faith), the mention of an established religion may appear to assert a hierarchy of faiths:

> 'The Church of England *being the established church* has a particular place – we have in the past and we still have a particular voice in Parliament and in government as a whole and that voice is a voice that represents the whole community and not just our own worshipping community.'
>
> (Church of England director of education)

The Catholic executive secretary of the Diocesan Schools Commission, Canon ——, also indicated a wish to respond to children of the faith:

'We are basically there for Catholic children whose parents have adherence to the faith. They may not be the greatest practising parents but they want their children to be educated in the context of the faith.'

He explained how a wish to respond to others in the communities had emerged:

'In the early seventies, where the communities were changing and the immigrants were coming in and our numbers were going down, the Archbishop of the time . . . said, "If you've got room to fit some of the Afro-Caribbean or the Asian population in," because again it's contrary to what Catholic schools are all about to be paragons of white faces in the community which has already become a very mixed sort of community . . .

'So, like St —— is right in the middle of the Asian community, they're half and half. The governors guided by the diocese have made that decision. It's a Catholic school, run on Catholic principles. The staff are Catholic, RE is all Catholic. The community actually love it and are clamouring to get in. The governors have made the decision that they are quite happy to have quite a high percentage of Afro-Caribbean and Asian pupils around the place.'

(Catholic executive secretary)

There is a suggestion here of a pragmatic modification of philosophy in response to changed circumstances.

A stronger version of the wish for Catholic and Church of England schools to serve neighbourhoods rather than faiths was put by other informants. The head of the Catholic 'exclusion prevention unit' felt that the purpose of Catholic schools had changed:

'Catholic education . . . was set up because Catholics were disenfranchised and there was a ghetto mentality. . . . It was necessary. Now Catholics are accepted into society and the only thing you can't do is marry Prince Charles, and that's OK by most people.

'"Catholic" means "universal", and universal means "all-encompassing". So if it's all-encompassing, which means "all-forgiving and accepting of everybody", then we are here to serve all of the people.

'There are a large number of Catholic schools that serve the area in which they find themselves. So for example St —— [in one of the most deprived areas of the city] has a very deliberate policy of saying we will include on our roll a large number of pupils who are not Catholic who may be of other faiths and other cultures because that is what the community here needs. They need a school which serves them. A lot of schools are similar.

'During the masses . . . and other services, the priest would be very careful to say, "Let us now pray to the God in which we believe", which would allow other children to be there and find a place in that, without taking part in the mass.'

However, she seemed to express a milder form of the same tension, evident in the views of the diocesan authorities, between the desire to serve a neighbourhood and to maintain the Catholic nature of Catholic education, an 'us' including 'them'. For her, 'Catholic education is very important':

'We are here to serve the community. So if you're a parent choosing a Catholic school for your child, you will understand that there will be times when we will be in community and we would be praying to God. We would prefer it if your child did not feel excluded from that, did not exclude himself or herself, but obviously you have the right to do that. But would this school be the right place for you to choose, if your child was going to feel excluded?'

Nevertheless, the head teacher of School A appeared to go further. She saw her school as playing a key role in the life of the whole community, as being 'at the forefront of bringing together the people of different faiths'. On her arrival as deputy head teacher twenty years previously, she had not yet formulated her view of the school's central place in the community:

'All [the governors] seemed to be interested in here was, 'was I a confirmed member of the Church of England?' That seemed to be the priority. I'm sure I hadn't thought it out at that time, but it's certainly been my view for a very long time now, a very long time . . . we see our role as enabling Christian children to have instruction in the Christian faith which we make provision for through services in church, confirmation for those who want it, *but we see it as just as important to enhance the understanding of all of the children in their various faiths.*'

Again there is a suggestion that by responding to children of all faiths one is responding to all children. Nevertheless, the view of the head teacher was backed by the governors, the school trustees, as well as the diocesan director of education, though she did not think such support extended to most on the diocesan board, who 'have a vision of a Church of England school which we do not fit'. She contrasted her view that a school should serve all the faiths in the community with that in Catholic schools: '[They] wouldn't share my view because they see their role very differently. They see their role as instructing their children in the Catholic faith.'

This misrepresented the variety of opinions expressed to me by those working locally in the Catholic system, and I found this to be a feature of my interviews with Anglicans: that the Anglican position was set out in contrast to that of Catholics. Yet the portrayal of Catholic education was close to the view of the governors and trustees of School C. The head teacher of that school identified the Catholic 'mission' of the school as 'first and foremost . . . to serve the Catholic population'. He felt that the priests who served the school were concerned to 'nurture the children's Catholic faith' and would have seen this as threatened by dilution of the school population by too many non-Catholics; 'they would, for example, be very unwilling to increase much more than at present the number of non-Catholics that will come into the school':

> 'They see the school as very much a Catholic school serving the needs of the Catholic community welcoming non-Catholics into the school on the basis that they are happy to be part of the Catholic ethos of the school and take a full part in the life of the school.'

This view was echoed by the school's RE coordinator, who thought the preparation for the sacraments of confession and confirmation would make it impractical to increase the numbers of non-Catholic students there: 'I would say, "Yes, keep our Catholic schools Catholic." In a predominantly white neighbourhood, slowly becoming more ethnically mixed, such a remark may take on a different complexion.

One of my informants from the Muslim Liaison Committee argued that in Islamic schools he 'would not say no Jew or Christian should be admitted [but] I want the whole structure and perspective Islamic'. The Islamic school was established to serve a community of Muslims rather than a neighbourhood of all faiths. Out of 108 children in the primary school 106 are from Muslim families. The parents of the other two opted for the school because they saw it as providing a more 'disciplined' education than in other schools. The school draws children from a wide area of the city, although '60–70 per cent of the students come from within a two-mile radius'. In fact, as with other schools established in the heart of a community of the faithful or the potentially faithful, in a predominantly Muslim area, the Islamic school also claimed to serve this *local* community. When the school had to survive on fees, there had been a considerable effort within the community to ensure that poorer families could be funded. As reported by the head teacher:

> 'There's quite a lot of unemployment in the area and that meant that the children had to be supported by the business community or the professional community or other working people. It's never been thought

of as a private school. It's always been regarded as a community school by the area and that's the reason there's so much help for each other.'

Applying the selection criteria

The admissions criteria for School I gave priority to practising Muslims and then they accepted 'anyone else, like Catholics'. With government funding it changed its selection criteria, placing a greater emphasis on distance from the school. Given the waiting list of 1500 applications for fifty new places in the expanded school, there was very little pressure to take in non-Muslims, however many applied to the school. They said that they did not and would not apply 'a quota' for non-Muslims, a term which appeared to have a harshness for some of my informants.

The Church of England diocesan authorities similarly insisted that they do not operate quotas at any school but operate 'preferential selection to Church of England families' in a few of their voluntary aided schools:

> 'We've asked all schools to consider admissions on the basis of distance from school, but there are some schools where this wouldn't work and would leave the connected worshipping community with youngsters that couldn't go to the school. So in a few pockets where there is a very strong worshipping community those who belong to the worshipping community get preferential treatment . . .
>
> 'Only half a dozen [schools] use their rights to put it first on their list but only four need to. If the other two did their sums they would realize they would get the same youngsters in, even if it wasn't number one.
>
> '*It's not a quota at all*. There are some schools where we exercise our admissions prerogative to favour worshipping families. . . . *We don't exclude families, no, no, no.*'
>
> (Church of England director of education)

But if a school is turning away on the basis of religion children who live nearby in favour of others living further away this could be described as exclusion.

The admissions criteria for School A did give 'priority to Christian children' though they also say that the school should be a community with a religious basis, serving all faiths. As the head teacher explained, after 'children who attend St ——'s church, which is very few' are 'children who attend other Christian churches', then 'children who are attenders at the temples and mosques of other faiths'. Many of the Christian students were not Anglican. According to the head of religious education, they were 'perhaps predominantly Roman Catholic, some of them are ex-travellers or fairground families . . . who are generally of Irish origin so they tend to be Catholic'. However, because the school was not oversubscribed, the school was able to accept all the non-Christian children who applied.

For the head teacher, problems might arise if the school increased in popularity. She had discussed this with the governors and board of trustees, who felt that in such circumstances they might have to change their admission criteria and introduce '*a quota on the Christian children* in order to keep a multi-faith school where there was a balanced community of all faiths'. However she recognized that this could be problematic: 'Luckily it hasn't happened.'

In contrast, the head teacher of the Catholic school openly acknowledged the existence and significance of a quota of non-Catholics at his school:

> 'There is a quota of a maximum of 10 per cent non-Catholics, established according to Regulation 666 of the 1996 Education Act, and the school has reached that maximum. According to the admission criteria, 'If there is a class of thirty children and thirty-five Catholics want a place then no non-Catholics would get a place.'

Responding to changing rolls

What happens when there is a decline in the number of children of the communities around schools committed to serving a particular faith? Schools may take the opportunity to rethink their philosophy, they may resist change and be threatened with closure, or they may change their rhetoric in order to remain viable without undergoing any deeper transformation. For School I, the possibility of a fall in demand for places seemed remote. In contrast, the head teacher of School A felt that she had made a shift in philosophy many years previously. She felt that a failure to respond to new circumstances had been a major factor in the demise of one of the Church of England secondary schools:

> 'It tried to ignore the fact that the context in which it was working had changed ... enormously. They were still trying to run a Christian academic school when by then a whole lot of features in the inner city had changed.'

School C had recently reached its quota of non-Catholics. This fact was beginning to exercise the minds of its governors and trustees and was causing considerable discomfort. It had a non-denominational nursery, accepting children on the basis of age and distance from the school, which resulted in a mix of faiths and backgrounds. In the past, although some of the non-Catholic children in the nursery had applied for a reception place, they had been unlikely to get in: 'Two years ago we would have thirty-five to forty Catholics wanting thirty places; now we've gone well below thirty suddenly.'

Falling rolls create financial problems for schools, funded according to the number of pupils. Admitting non-Catholic children from the nursery and elsewhere could have resolved this problem, but a relaxation of the admissions criteria would have changed the character of the school, as the head teacher reported:

> 'In terms of non-Catholics, [in the past] thirty apply and maybe one or two might get in if they have got an older brother or sister in the school. This year [more] would get in *but the governors have their criteria which would only allow three to come in.*
>
> 'There's a dilemma there. Is it convenient to take non-Catholic children just to keep your budget up? Or is it something where you say "No, we are a Catholic school, we will ride the storm, and maybe we'll find other Catholic parents who will find out there are places here and hopefully then we'll be in a situation where we'll have rising numbers not falling rolls."

It was unclear how the school was resolving this 'dilemma'. The head teacher gave me two different versions, perhaps accounted for by his ambivalence about 'talking down' the school to an outsider and by a distinction he drew between what the governors might say they were doing officially and what they might do in practice: 'The governors can't change the criteria for . . . next year . . . [but] of course what the governors do informally is an entirely different matter.'

Resolution 1

TB: There has been this concern about falling rolls?

Head teacher: There is now, yes.

TB: That is a current burning issue?

Head teacher: Yes, it is.

TB: Could the school be threatened with closure?

Head teacher: Absolutely yes.

I was told that the governors had decided to take more non-Catholics into the reception class: 'Four or five next year'. They aimed to compensate for this increase in the proportion of non-Catholic children lower down the school by making changes higher up:

> 'The view of the governors is that they will have to make a few changes to compensate for *what they are losing* in reception class in terms of numbers by increasing the size of the classes up the school, provided that if they do go over what we call their standard number [of] thirty the children coming into the thirty-first or thirty-second place are *Catholic.*'

However, the arithmetic of this 'short-term solution' creates its own problems. Taking more non-Catholic children into the reception year creates a knock-on effect in future years, and the head teacher is concerned about the implications of such a policy: 'If the school decides suddenly to say, "Yes we'll let you in," and then says "We won't guarantee your brother or sister [a place]," I don't think that's particularly Christian.'

Resolution 2

TB: Has that issue [of the threat of school closure] been raised?

Head teacher: No, not now, the school is popular.

In the second version, the head attributed to others the kind of solution to the prospect of diminishing numbers of Catholic children which he had previously attributed to his own school. For example, after saying that the governors might be attracted by some arrangement that breached the admission criteria, informally, he added in response to my request for clarification:

'I think there would be some Catholic schools where they would say, "What others don't know doesn't harm them." They may simply say, "Well, we will take a few extra non-Catholics into the school." I don't think that will happen here. . . . I think they'll bite the bullet as it were and say, "We will have to tighten our belts for a year or two in the hope that things change." Whereas in some Catholic schools, they would say, "It's only one more."

'The [school] will be courageous and say, "maybe we're going to have less resources for a few years", "You may have to have staff changes", if you've got temporary contracts, we may have to say, "We can't continue to provide the right support for a class teacher because we simply can't afford the salary." I think they may be prepared to do these things to retain the Catholic character of the school.'

He thought that there might be ways of attracting Catholic pupils to the school from further afield:

'I think the governors may take the view that there are other Catholic schools with similar problems close to us perhaps worse and maybe we'll attract a few of their parents here. . . . It's a competitive situation out there. We've got to live in that competitive situation.'

However, attracting Catholics to the school from other areas could be a fraught matter: 'The priests will talk to each other about this. . . . If a priest feels his school is threatened he might tell the neighbouring priest to keep his hands off his parents.'

Resolution 3?

Irrespective of the popularity of the school or its reaction to falling rolls, the head teacher was not going to have to face the future of this school himself: he was moving to become head teacher of a different, larger Catholic school with a more mixed population and a more open attitude to other faiths and cultures. He saw this openness as helping to address problems of equal opportunities and racism which he felt were unaddressed at his present school. He was, however, at pains to continue a distinction between '*our* Catholic children' and the others:

> 'I'm moving to another school where there is more of a welcome and a respect; that we're not frightened of what other children bring into school provided it doesn't confuse *our Catholic children* in their faith. I think that's where I draw the line.
>
> 'There are far more non-Catholics coming to that school – Afro-Caribbeans – Christian probably, but not Catholic. There are going to be children of different faiths. . . . I would be looking forward to the challenge . . . in relation to trying to help the Catholic children, the Christian children come to a deeper understanding of other cultures. . . . I do feel that if we don't do that we will not help *our children, our Catholic children*, when they leave this school to develop a respect for other cultures.'

All the faithful?

When my informants talked of serving a faith or a neighbourhood, did they mean *all* of the faithful or *all* in the neighbourhood, irrespective of attainment, impairment or behaviour, for example? The representatives of the Catholic and Church of England education authorities both expressed a commitment to a comprehensive philosophy which they counterposed to the competitive, market imperatives which were compounding selection by attainment in grammar schools in the city. For the Church of England diocesan director of education:

> 'In terms of private schools there's nothing you can do . . . but unfortunately private education undermines what the state can offer. . . . [I] would not be in favour of the continuation of grammar schools. This is not a board view because we have not discussed it, but I favour a school community that represents the community at large. Because I think there are some important lessons to be learnt about communities

which you can only get to grips with if you have a true mixed comprehensive, ideally with total inclusion.'

The reference here is to the *inclusion* of students with impairments or otherwise categorized as 'having special needs'. The head teacher of School I felt that disability or educational difficulty should not be a barrier to the inclusion of children at her school: 'We would include anybody.' However, the Muslim Liaison Committee measured the success of their Saturday schools in terms of the numbers of children who had been helped to pass their examinations for grammar schools:

> 'Every year eight to ten pass the eleven plus and go to the grammar school. I have produced – with the help of Almighty God he has chosen me to look after – 111 children who have passed the eleven-plus who have gone to the grammar schools.'

School A showed its commitment to including people with disabilities by the support it gave to staff who were ill or had an impairment. One teacher unable to write had a full-time assistant. In terms of their admission criteria, they gave priority to 'children with special needs' over 'brothers and sisters and distance'. According to the head teacher, giving priority to such students was supported generally by the staff, following 'deep discussion'.

The Catholic diocesan executive secretary explained too that 'our philosophy is inclusive', though he felt that sometimes practice within the LEA lagged behind the views of students themselves:

> 'If a parent or child wants to come to a Catholic school then we will try our hardest to take them. . . . If there is such an extent of disability that the authority would say we can't put in the resources behind it . . . then we would talk with the parents and the child and perhaps say that a special school would be better. But what is interesting is that a lot of our children are saying to us: "Well, blow my disability, I want to be in a normal school."'

The head teacher of the Catholic exclusions prevention unit wanted schools to extend their tolerance to students whom they saw as disciplinary problems, who were too frequently seen as beyond forgiveness or redemption:

> 'If we say we are Christians, then "Christian" means that we include everybody because Christ came to call everyone. . . . As soon as a child was permanently excluded from a Catholic school we were almost saying you aren't good enough to be a Catholic, which isn't very Christian.'

The head teacher of School C argued that Catholic education involved conveying a belief in community service, to reach out to those 'in need'. However, he did not extend this to a philosophical commitment to inclusion in the mainstream of children with impairments. He linked the acceptance of a child to the availability of resources. The school was not wheelchair-accessible although it was on a single-storey site and would not accept children in wheelchairs.

> 'I think most Catholic schools would take a very practical look at this. [If] . . . we don't have what they need . . . we would not do it. On the other hand, if we were going to be given the resources we would seriously consider it.'

This conditional welcome was in evidence in the acceptance on roll of a child with Down's syndrome:

> 'He comes from a *devout* Catholic family. They were *desperately* keen for him to come to us, and they do have a certain amount of influence within the parish, and I as his head teacher and my staff felt that their notion of their "gift from God", as they describe John, was something they wanted to share with *normal* children; would help *normal* children to look upon Down's syndrome children in a different way. There are issues there linked to abortion, we respected entirely. But at the same time we were not prepared for John to come into the school without the level of support that would be needed for him to receive an education. We did not see it as the role of the school to provide a childminding service. This is an educational establishment. . . . We insisted that he had a statement of his needs, and the parents didn't want that. In the end they did, because that was the only way the school was going to be able to help John. We take a very practical view.
>
> 'It's a tremendous experience to work in a school with a Down's syndrome child for all of us. I've learnt such a lot, and he is making progress within the school. . . . If there comes a time when John's progress is so limited – and he is already operating two years below his peer group now – then clearly we would have to say, maybe it was right for John to go somewhere else.'

THE DEMAND FOR ISLAMIC SCHOOLS

My informants saw the establishment of Islamic schools as a reaction to the failure on the part of state schools to respond to the needs of their children; to respect their identities; to properly include them. The group of six professional women who were instrumental in getting the Islamic primary school off the ground were concerned, according to the head teacher, that 'the structure wasn't there to help our children to develop confidence as Muslims'. Some had been through the English state system themselves and wanted their pupils to avoid the shortcomings of their own education. However, when they visited schools they felt that their identities and individuality were still disregarded. In the past teachers 'did not want to know' what their needs were; now they made assumptions about their needs before they had got to know them:

> 'For example, one particular school . . . the sort of thing that we heard was "Oh, we have a lot of classroom assistants so that we can speak to the child in their home language. I assume that will be either Punjabi or Urdu." There were assumptions being made . . . that the child would not be speaking fluent English when they came into school. And also about clothes: "It's all right to wear a shalwar kameez." Making assumptions on the basis of the stated religion that they would want to wear a shalwar kameez rather than more Western dress.'

The members of the Muslim Liaison Committee were concerned about their children's lack of progress and low admissions into higher education. In response, the Muslim communities had established a large building to house the weekend classes, which had been running in less suitable accommodation for twelve years, and for 'teacher training classes organized by local schools'. They, too, thought low achievement was related to problems of identity, but felt it was blamed – wrongly – on language difficulties: 'The teachers say, "What can we do?" This is their second language.' In their experience, the children's use of their mother tongue was diminishing rapidly, and this was particularly evident in the mosque:

> 'We have to hire a special imam to come and give a sermon on religion in English because our children do not understand our language. The children who are over twenty-five, they might; but below twenty-five, they don't understand our language.'

Concerns over representation

One informant, who was chair of governors of a large school with only 4 per cent of non-Muslim pupils, argued that if schools with a mainly Muslim population were run by the Muslim parents and had more Muslim teachers then they 'would be as good as any Christian schools'. Yet 60 per cent of his fellow governors were non-Muslim. He saw that there were problems of recruitment when many Muslims were 'not very conversant with the education system'. Some Muslim governors were not reappointed because they were in 'the extreme group' or were 'not up to standard', but others just did not ' play the game' according to English rules:

'My nomination has been recommended, and somehow or other I've behaved myself so it has been extended, but the people who didn't behave, their names were struck off.'

'It's very important to speak the language of the host community. The language is not only the English language but the way hypocrisy is shown. We've got to be hypocrites to fight for our cause.'

They were looking for an effective partnership with the local education authority in providing support and training for new governors:

'I am not saying plenty of educated Muslims are available . . . But we are the taxpayer . . . If there is sincerity, if there is a will, there is a way.'

Concern about the curriculum

In relation to curriculum content, the chair of governors thought he had won 'limited' concessions from the school and local education authority. There was a non-Christian assembly, and no sex education, but he felt that with such a majority of Muslims the assembly should be based on the Muslim faith. He had a continuing concern about the teaching of aspects of art and music that he saw as forbidden within Islam (see Muslim Educational Trust 1997). However, the head teacher had insisted that addressing this was impossible within the national curriculum. He and others commented on requirements for modesty for both boys and girls, which became particularly important for secondary students. They wanted to alter the arrangements for changing and showering after PE, and pointed out that many non-Muslim students feel uncomfortable about the expectation of communal nudity.

The demand for single-sex education

The refusal of many Muslim parents to send their daughters to mixed secondary schools and the lack of places in single-sex ones were given as principal arguments for the expansion of Islamic schools (see also Haw 1998). According to my informants from the Muslim Liaison Committee, girls were 'being denied equal opportunities'. These Muslim parents, like many others, felt obliged to send their female children to private schools:

'We paid because our faith does not allow the girls when they are reaching the age of puberty to mix. Once they are grown up they are mature, they understand what is wrong and right, then OK they can protect and save themselves, but not at that tender age when they do not know and they can be influenced by the environment.'

This option of private education was not open to poorer families, and it was felt that the Council had not come to terms with the realities of life in the Muslim communities, where large numbers of girls were either withdrawn from school or sent back to family in Pakistan. These girls tended to 'marry very young' and the marriages were 'unstable': 'That's why I say the government has not really studied what is the actual requirement.'

There had been a long-standing campaign for an increase in the number of girls-only places at secondary schools, which had been seen, originally, as a more realistic option than trying to get state funding for a Muslim school. However, as in other negotiations with the Council, they felt there had been an absence of 'sincerity'. They thought agreement with the education authority had been obtained, and then the decision had been reversed by a change in the rules of the game. At first a decision was to depend on a poll of the parents of three schools affected by a change to single-sex education:

'The parents agreed, and when the parents agreed they said we should ask even the students who are studying there what they want. Then they asked these girls. [They were] interviewed, I remember, on television, and they said "No, no, we live in this country . . . and our parents are a bit primitive, we don't want it." They took the decision, [that] "if the students are not happy then why should we force them?" And then the question was closed.'

They saw this consultation with students over school choice as less than even-handed given the rhetoric on *parental* choice in decisions about school admissions.

Variations of view

As the consultation over secondary schools showed, there were different attitudes to religious observance within the Muslim communities. Some adults did not see the division of the sexes at secondary level as essential either, preferring to tell young people the rules and 'trust' them. There were also differences about how Islamic schools should be run. My two informants from the Muslim Liaison Committee had a particular attachment to a large Islamic school in the city which they would have preferred to receive state funding, and had reservations about the school I visited. A member of the group, who worked to establish School I, argued that this attitude did not reflect fundamental theological differences but might have a gender dimension. She thought that the Muslim Liaison Committee mixed in 'a predominantly male circle' and the school they favoured was 'much more male-dominated':

'I often say that this school is female-dominated and the mothers are very active in it. That in itself [creates] certain differences, doesn't it? . . . You have to have a good sense of humour, you know [laughs] . . . it doesn't create any problems or tensions as such.'

She felt that this female perspective added something to the educational opportunities for girls:

'It is not a difference in terms of view. But I do feel that being female as teachers and a lot of mothers being involved there is a lot more sensitivity to the needs of girls. . . . The mothers know what they have been through and are quite keen to ensure that the girls have an opportunity to go into higher education and to go into professions. I am not remotely suggesting that the males wouldn't have the same desires but not having gone through the same problems.'

A different set of reasons for supporting the development of Islamic schools came from Muslims working within the educational administration, who felt that Islamic schools were likely to promote multicultural under-standing by mediating the more extreme views of religious leaders:

'Are we going to say, yes, religions can continue and prosper at family level or at the mosque or religious place [but not at school]? But that is even more dangerous because then you are abdicating your responsibility as a society, leaving a person in the hands of those people who are not qualified to give the right type of approach in religion which will allow a person to live in a society which is a multi-culture.'

REACTIONS TO THE ISLAMIC SCHOOL

The state funding of an Islamic school and the possibility of more such schools stimulated the expression of views about Islamic schools as well as faith schools in general. When the Islamic school was being established, there was considerable support from other religious organizations: Hindu, Christian and Jewish. However, there was some opposition, from those who said they feared *an increase* in the fragmentation of education. However, as people recognized that 'whatever law there is has to be applied equally' they started to argue that 'we should get rid of all religious-based schools and have one unified system'.

An opposition to all faith schools was put forward by a teacher from the Sikh community: 'Segregation . . . is not integrating, it is not uniting the nation. In religious schools you are not actually teaching patriotism for the whole nation but to their own faith and community.'

Yet he had particular reservations about the development of Islamic schools, which he thought would accelerate the development of a Muslim population without close ties to the rest of the nation. He saw Muslims as having large families – 'fifteen, twenty children' – and thought that 'in another fifty years' time it may be the majority in this country': 'We are waiting for the disaster which. . . . It's a small island, it's natural resources are very limited, and if . . . division or tension rises in the future . . . and interests are narrow then there will be problems for the whole country.'

Both the Catholic and Church of England authorities acknowledged the justice of the Muslim argument for equal rights. Canon —— recognized that 'If Catholic parents have been given this wonderful facility, then this should be open to parents of other faiths', adding the caveat that 'the school must conform to all needs of the national curriculum'. Now my questioning should have been more incisive at that point given the theological difficulties that Muslims have in some areas of the curriculum, so I am not sure whether the remark referred specifically to these prohibitions. However, he did wonder whether the Muslims themselves or other religious groups really wanted separate schools:

> 'Over twenty years in [a different city] it was most interesting talking to the Indian parents. . . . Many of them and the children wanted what they would call "a normal school" . . . whether a Catholic school or the school next door or whatever. They didn't want to go to a heavily Hindu or Muslim school because they felt they were going to get their faith chucked at them and their children were already part of a multicultural background. . . . They were more than happy to be educated in the system in that city and send their children to the mosque or the temple like we send our children to church.'

It is interesting that Catholic and, presumably, Anglican schools are seen as 'normal', but not those of other religious denominations. In his study of demands for Muslim schools in Bradford, Halstead (1988), too, reported a range of views within the Muslim community about the desirability of Islamic schools. But in this city the overall demand for such education is clear.

The Church of England diocesan director was very concerned about fragmentation of the system. His concern about Islamic schools echoed the objections to the support for Christian faith schools in the 1944 Education Act: 'I think it actually makes the whole thing very difficult for the LEA to manage' (Chadwick 1997). He distinguished Muslim schools, which he thought would contribute to the creation of 'very inward-looking communities', from the outward-looking view of Church of England schools:

> 'Whereas . . . we have Muslims sending their children to Church of England schools and Sikhs sending their children to Church of England

schools. . . . I am not sure that . . . Christian parents would choose to send their children to a Muslim school and I'm not sure that the Sikh community would necessarily choose to send their children to a Muslim school.'

THE MULTIPLICATION OF DIVISION?

However, the head teacher of School A felt that she had to recognize the role played by existing faith schools like hers in the pressure from other religious communities for their own schools. The solution for divisiveness created by a proliferation of religious denomination schools was to end all such schools. However, she also revealed a barrier to such action, in the competitive relationship between the Anglicans and Catholics:

'If the existence of my school and others like it means that we're going to have more and more groups setting up their own schools, then *if the Catholics would go along with it* . . . personally, I would get rid of Church of England schools now. It's not a typical view . . . but I feel so strongly that the only way forward is to educate children together which we do here. . . . I think that gives an opportunity for increased understanding.

'But the penalty for us being here is going to be more and more initially Islamic schools. I suspect that will only be the beginning. I think we might get pressure from Hindus next . . . and for various sections of the Christian community for different types of schools. We could end up with a situation where more and more children go to segregated schools where they don't meet the general run of the population. I think that's really bad for the pupils and I feel very strongly about it. . . . There's going to be greater and greater division.'

Even in schools actively attempting to include the students in the neighbourhood, selective pressures, particularly at secondary school, may frustrate their aims. In the Church of England secondary, there was a considerable preponderance of boys and the head teacher remarked how the lack of girls was lowering the school's position on league tables 'because of the underachievement of boys': 'In some years it has been even worse, we have actually had a whole boys' tutor group. . . . This is a problem shared by three or four of the local schools.'

This gender imbalance is characteristic of mixed schools in predominantly Muslim areas. This is a further way in which selection by religion may have an effect on the way both schools of and not of the faith relate to their communities. The Catholic secondary school to which many children were expected to transfer from School C had responded to its changing population by increasing its ethnic mix. In this city, as in other areas where schools have a large number of students with a Muslim background, there is a tendency for both white and Afro-Caribbean students to congregate in Christian faith schools; the Catholic secondary school nearest to School C was developing this mix. However, according to the head teacher of School C, the white community surrounding the school was characterized by 'deeply rooted racism'. The racist attitudes of parents of children at his school were affecting recruitment at the secondary school and thus putting it under threat. A 'significant number' of parents did not send their children there 'because of the presence of Afro-Caribbean children'. Now, the head teacher said at one point that this reluctance was because 'they associate Afro-Caribbean boys particularly with bad behaviour'. But it seems that the 'racism' of parents itself was accounting for their 'bad behaviour', just as the wider racism in schools and categorization procedures may account for the disciplinary conflict and perceptions of behaviour of Afro-Caribbean students.

Despite the wishes of some there is likely to be a continuing expansion of Islamic schools in the city. My Sikh informant thought that, eventually, there would be an unstoppable pressure within his own community for separate schools:

> 'If there is a tendency in the country as a whole that every faith has its own schools, then you have to have for your survival. . . . If the trend continues – the Muslims have their schools the Jews have their own schools, Christians have their schools – then at some point we have to say, "Yes, we will have our own schools."'

The Catholic diocesan authorities are eager to maintain the status quo of their schools, though they do envisage that in the future not all parishes may be able to sustain a primary school. A Catholic sixth-form college closed due to lack of demand, but they were negotiating with the local authority to add sixth forms to all of their secondary schools. With the problem of falling rolls in secondary schools, and the issues of fragmentation that he raised, did the Church of England diocesan director of education anticipate a reduction in the numbers of Church of England schools? 'Oh no. We're actually looking for expansion. We actually believe we have something special to offer.'

RELIGION INTO INCLUSION WON'T GO?

My informants set out for me a dilemma between religious denomination schools serving a community of the faithful and serving the communities in their locality. Some prioritized the role of the religious denomination schools in serving a neighbourhood. But it is difficult for faith schools to avoid creating a hierarchy of membership, for students of the faith, those of other faiths and those of no faith. There were clear expressions of such hierarchies in my interviews. I did not have space to report in detail on the way these and other faith schools affect the participation of staff, although the existence of faith schools restricts the possibilities for appointment and promotion in an area, particularly for teachers and other staff without a particular faith.

The head teacher of School I, thought that in the coming years a network of Islamic schools would develop, more closely related to a neighbourhood. It is possible that changes in the composition of such neighbourhoods and in religious commitment within the Muslim communities might eventually present some of these schools with the same dilemmas as those faced by Anglican and Catholic schools.

Any study of religious communities in England cannot ignore the way Muslims, the Islamic religion and nations practising it, are seen as 'alien' or 'other' by many people. Such attitudes make it difficult for people to listen carefully to their views or to apply the law and local opportunities equitably. The delay in funding Islamic schools was seen to reflect an unwillingness to grant the same choices to Muslims as other religions. But they felt that they had a considerable struggle to gain the same level of recognition in education as other faiths: 'It's all political. [Muslim schools] would not have got recognition if there were not the two other schools that the Jewish lobby wanted recognition for in London somewhere.'

There may be reticence in acknowledging the extent to which Muslims feel that their faith and cultural identities are given less than full respect within the city's education system. Responding to the issues raised about gender, the relationship between religious teachings and the national curriculum, the representation of Muslims on governing bodies seemed an essential stage in the building of good community relationships. The Muslim population experience cultural exclusion, and this fuels a desire to protect and affirm their identity in separate schools.

The development of Islamic schools was represented to me as a way of ensuring that Muslim children could grow up to be productive citizens: 'They will be good citizens in this society . . . we are not looking for ourselves, we are looking for a better Britain'. Selection by religion is portrayed by these informants – as by Anglican and Catholic archbishops – as a means of promoting inclusion in society. A similar argument is sometimes advanced by those who regard a separate special education for pupils with impairments or otherwise categorized as having 'special educational needs' as the best preparation for a productive and fulfilling participation in adult life.

But can selection by religion, (or other forms of selection), reduce devaluation and division within communities? In a competitive system, the possibility of selection by faith can conceal selection by popular schools in relation to attainment and ethnicity. In schools where there are concentrations of students from Afro-Caribbean, Bangladeshi, Pakistani or Indian backgrounds there tends to be an under-representation of white students compared to their proportion in the local population: there is ethnic flight. There is little doubt that in this city, as elsewhere, the existence of faith schools interacts with and exacerbates ethnic divisions as well as other forms of selection. Increasing the separation of communities along religious and ethnic lines – where there is already considerable potential for conflict – makes the resolution of that conflict more difficult.

The Church of England diocese was trying to provide guidelines for the running of Anglican faith schools that would make them welcoming to students irrespective of faith. They found it difficult to express what would distinguish such schools from non-faith schools.

> 'When we show people our diocesan expectations, one of the arguments that comes back from many of our head teachers is "We do that, but that's what you expect of any school," and we say, "Of course, that's what you expect of any school, but its the plus, it's the bit extra, that's important."'

There are lessons from faith schools for all schools. Perhaps in all schools attention should be given to living by shared values of respect and equity, to the building of collaborating communities, to the nurturing of the human spirit of staff and students. This is part of the meaning I would give to inclusion. Spirituality and a commitment to moral values are not the property of religion. But the existence of faith schools may contribute to a reticence on the part of other schools when it comes to an open expression of those values which make life worthwhile.

But if the 'bit extra' is defined, in a way that cannot apply to any school, in a more specifically Anglican or Catholic or Islamic way, it may make a difference between the nature of participation within the school of those of and not of the faith, both students and staff. The position of the Church of England as the established faith, encourages the expression of a hierarchy of faiths as well as of national identities within Britain. Further as the head teacher of School A passionately pointed out, the existence of some religious-denomination schools constantly fuels the demand for others. It reduces the potential for schools to serve all the students within mixed neighbourhoods, as well as encouraging the physical and cultural segregation of members of different ethnic groups.

REFERENCES

Archbishops' Council (2000) *Church Schools Review Group*, chaired by Lord Dearing, London: Archbishops' Council.

Asian Youth Movement (1983) *Policy Statement on Religious/Separate Schools*, Bradford: Asian Youth Movement.

Bunting, M. (2001) 'Children in the Frontline', *Guardian*, 7 September 2001.

Chadwick, P. (1994) *Schools of Reconciliation*, London: Cassell.

Chadwick, P. (1997) *Shifting Alliances, Church and State in English Education*, London: Cassell.

Department for Education and Employment (1996) Education Act, London: HMSO.

Halstead, J.M. (1986) *The Case for Muslim Voluntary Aided Schools: Some Philosophical Reflections*, Cambridge: Islamic Academy.

Halstead, J.M. (1988) *Education Justice and Cultural Diversity; An Examination of the Honeyford Affair, 1984–5*, London: Falmer Press.

Haw, K. (1998) *Educating Muslim Girls; Shifting Discourses*, Milton Keynes: Open University Press.

Hickman, M. (1995) *Religion, Class and Identity; the State, the Catholic Church and the Education of the Irish in Britain*, Aldershot: Avebury.

Home Office (2001) Community Cohesion: A Report of the Independent Review Team, chaired by Ted Cantle, London: Home Office.

McLenahan, C., Cairns, E., Dunn, S. and Morgan, V. (1993) 'Planned Integrated and Desegregated Schools in Northern Ireland,' *Irish Journal of Education*, (XXVII), 50–59.

Murray, D., Smith A. and Birthistle, U. (1997) *Education in Ireland*, University of Limerick: Irish Peace Institute Research Centre.

Muslim Educational Trust (1997) 'Comments on the Government White Paper, Excellence in Schools,' London: Muslim Educational Trust.

National Union of Teachers (1984) *Religious Education in a Multi-faith Society*, London: NUT.

Simon, B. (1991) *Education and the Social Order*, London: Lawrence and Wishart.

Waines, D. (1995) *An Introduction to Islam*, Cambridge: Cambridge University Press.

Chapter 6

Single-sex education and inclusive school communities

Patricia Potts and Gwenn Edwards

INTRODUCTION

This chapter is the result of a collaboration between a member of the research team and a local Birmingham practitioner. At the time of writing this chapter one of us was working as an inclusion officer in the city. This gave her an insight into the culture of the Education Department as a whole, as well as into specific strategies aimed at moving towards a more inclusive ethos. Her interest in single-sex education arose primarily from her professional role. However, when the time came to choose a secondary school for her son, it became clear that there were issues relating to inclusion that the city had not yet addressed. If her son went to what was described as a 'comprehensive' school, it was likely that he would end up being taught in all-boys classes due to the small number of girls in the school, a consequence of its close proximity to a very large girls' school.

As an insider, she was well placed to investigate the effect of gender imbalances on school communities because schools where she was known were pleased to cooperate in the project and to facilitate access to students. The questions we wanted to ask were:

1   What impact does being in a single-sex school have on students' learning?
2   How do single-sex schools counter gender imbalances?
3   How can single-sex schools increase participation and reduce exclusionary pressures?
4   What criteria do families use in choosing a secondary school?

STRUCTURE OF THE CHAPTER

Three maintained secondary schools participated in this project: a boys' school, a girls' school and a co-educational school, all within one area of the city. None of them are selective by competitive entry examination, but they all use setting by ability. After a review of recent research on single-sex education, we introduce the area and the schools. Then we present the views of the three head teachers and the perspectives of some of their students, as well as the view of a local parent who is also a teacher. We discuss the themes that emerge from these conversations, in relation both to our initial questions and the published literature. We conclude that single-sex education profoundly affects the capacity of secondary schools to develop as inclusive communities. Further, there are complex mechanisms at work in co-educational as well as in single-sex schools which perpetuate gender stereotyping, but it would appear that, so far, strategies for change are not linked to other commitments to social inclusion.

RECENT RESEARCH

Recent research on single-sex schooling gives us a context for investigating answers to our questions. Studies of single-sex compared with co-education and of the attainment of girls in single-sex settings conclude that:

> When attempts have been made to control statistically for differences in the ability and social class of intakes, the apparent discrepancy in exam performance between co-educational and single-sex schools largely disappears.
>
> (Smithers and Robinson 1997: 2)

> The general conclusion from this review is that there is no conclusive evidence that single-sex schooling is better than co-educational schooling.
>
> (Elwood and Gipps 1999: 55)

One of the assumptions underlying support for single-sex education, especially for girls, is that boys dominate in co-educational classrooms. This was evident in Pat Mahony's research in the 1980s (see Mahony 1985), but is not supported by more recent work: 'There was no support at all for the idea that boys tend to dominate classes' (Smithers and Robinson, op. cit. p.13).

Factors other than single sex are responsible for the academic success of single-sex schools. In their review of research for OFSTED, David Gillborn and Heidi Safia Mirza found that while girls outperform boys at GCSE level by nine percentage points, white students outperform black students by eighteen percentage points and students from non-manual backgrounds outperform students from manual backgrounds by forty-nine percentage points (Gillborn and Mirza 2000: 23, note 71): 'In contrast to the disproportionate media attention, our data shows gender to be a less problematic issue than the significant disadvantage of "race" and the even greater inequality of class' (op. cit. p.23);

Apart from the deceptive link between an all-girls' intake and high achievement, a combination of traditional (uniform, a secure environment) and progressive (non-stereotyped subject and career choices) characteristics may strengthen the appeal of single-sex schools for girls (see Ball and Gewirtz 1997; Elwood and Gipps, op. cit. p.47) even though this may not enable all girls to flourish: 'Single-sex education can be used for emancipation or oppression' (Kruse 1996, quoted in Murphy and Gipps 1996: 189; see also Ball and Gewirtz, op. cit.).

In their study of gender reform in Australian co-educational schools, Jane Kenway and her colleagues also challenge the orthodox assumption that single-sex settings benefit girls. The combination of feeling good about yourself, being ambitious and working hard can remain a fantasy if the 'material realities' of students' lives preclude making autonomous choices. Further, the safety associated with all-girls' settings can perpetuate myths of female virtue and helplessness. Students who participated in this project made a link between social justice and co-education:

> While girls recognise the value of single-sex, they also point out that mixed groups are needed too. Most girls suggest the flexible use of both but stress the importance of better co-education for the development of better understanding and relationships. . . . Those boys who indicated an enthusiasm for gender justice seem, like girls, to pin their hopes on co-education.
>
> (Kenway *et al.* 1998: 150, 163)

Both single-sex and co-educational settings may underestimate how different are the experiences of girls and boys in secondary schools. In their study of boys' underachievement in selective schools, Sally Power and her colleagues argue that schools that are selective by ability 'save' students from the disturbing effects of adolescence by making so many demands on their time that this 'insulates them from neighbourhood influences': 'It may be that comprehensive schools offer some boys a greater range of acceptable behaviours and looser boundaries between home and school that make the pressures and penalties of success and failure less severe' (Power *et al.* 1998: 149–150).

These looser boundaries may have other positive consequences: 'Pupils in co-educational schools have a more positive view of their schools' impact on their social and personal development and have less traditional views about work and family roles' (Elwood and Gipps, op. cit. p.52).

Researchers have a variety of perspectives on the relationship between gender, educational equalities and social inclusion. Some researchers make a connection between the social and organizational aspects of co-education and equitable relationships between young men and women. Others stress the reduction of inequalities in attainment as the way to achieve social justice.

The relationship between single-sex education and processes of inclusion is not simple and cannot be described independently of other, interrelated social factors.

INTRODUCTION TO THE AREA AND THE THREE SCHOOLS

The three schools are situated in two neighbouring wards to the south-west of the city (see map on page 16). The overall area is economically and culturally mixed. The co-educational school is in a ward with a wide range of housing, from fairly affluent, large detached houses in two conservation areas to houses where there are still outside toilets, and bathrooms shared by more than one family. Over seventy per cent of the housing is owner-occupied and just over a quarter of the population belong to black and other ethnic minority groups. Employment opportunities in the ward come from shops and banks within the two main shopping areas. Unemployment here is around 9 per cent, lower than the Birmingham average.

The boys' school and the girls' school are in a ward that is predominantly residential. Consequently, there are few employment opportunities. The largest employer is the city-wide bus company, which has a depot within the ward and the girls' school itself is the fourth highest local employer. Housing consists mainly of inter-war and post-war family homes, including high-rise flats. Half the houses are owner-occupied and the other half rented from the local authority. This area is predominantly white; less than seven per cent of the population belong to black and other ethnic minority groups.

There are sharp contrasts across the two wards. You can turn the corner of a street where detached houses sell for two hundred thousand pounds or more into a street with high-rise flats and properties boarded up. There are two large parks and a prestigious private golf club. The area as a whole has become very popular with professional people in the last decade, and this has boosted property prices. The population is quite mobile, as can be seen from the numbers of houses that are for sale. An indication of the popularity of this area is that the houses do not stay on the market for long.

The schools included in this study are not the only secondary schools in the area: there is also a Catholic school, another boys' school and a grammar school. Children from the seven primary schools in the immediate area do not necessarily transfer to these local secondary schools. Few secondaries have a single feeder primary school and some receive new students from up to fifty, indicating huge catchment areas.

In each of the three schools, about fifty per cent of the students do not have English as their first language. In the boys' school about two-thirds of the students were entitled to free school meals and in the co-educational school nearly half, though in each case the take-up was lower. These rates are much higher than the national average. In the girls' school, eligibility for free school meals was lower than for the co-educational school and low for the city, indicating a higher overall socio-economic status of families with daughters at the girls' school. Levels of attainment in all three schools were below the national average.

The boys' school

The boys' school has about 560 students aged from eleven to sixteen, including just under sixty with statements of special educational needs. It is a popular school, with a waiting list for Year 7. The school is situated just off an affluent residential road, with a drive leading to the 1930s building. The first impression of the school is one of horticulture: there are greenhouses and lots of plants lining the drive and entrance, making a very pleasant approach to the school's front entrance. Once inside, although the greenery continues, there is a feeling of isolation. Where do we go? Will anyone know we're here? The entrance foyer is austere and, as the welcome of the flowers fades, there's an atmosphere of order and discipline. There are a few plants and some notices about behaviour but no school photographs or evidence of students' activities and achievements.

The girls' school

The girls' school has 1,663 students on roll, making it one of the largest schools in the city and the largest single-sex school in Europe. Until the 1970s it was the girls' grammar school for the area. The local boys' grammar school is now co-educational. The size of the girls' school is partly a reflection of demographic changes that have occurred in the area over the last two decades, specifically the increase in the number of Asian families in the area. The majority of these are Muslim families who want single-sex education for their daughters.

The school is divided into lower and upper schools, with different buildings, and there is a separate canteen block. A sixth-form centre is also part of the school, again with its own building. The sixth form is mixed, but currently there are not any boys on roll, and over the years only a very small numbers of boys have attended the centre. There are six colleges of further education and four sixth-form colleges in the city, giving students a wide range of choice post-sixteen. Some of the girls in the school-based sixth-form centre are young women who might not continue with their education if there were not single-sex provision.

The school was awarded Beacon status in 1999, under the government's Excellence in Cities programme. The school was awarded this for several areas: expertise in most subject areas, reducing bureaucracy, specialist provision for extended learning (for students identified as 'gifted and talented'), staff development and, lastly, target-setting, monitoring and the evaluation of pupil progress.

The school is pleasantly situated in its own grounds and backs on to a park; it is approached along a tree-lined drive. The main reception area is situated in the upper school, which also houses other shared facilities such as the hall. The reception area is well signed and the foyer is welcoming, displaying information about various school activities. There are lots of photographs and awards. The head teacher and deputy have their offices just off this foyer and there is a waiting area outside.

The co-educational school

The co-educational school has a population of around 550 students, aged between eleven and sixteen, with a girl–boy ratio of one to three. Over the last two years this school has established a close relationship with a secondary special school for students classified as having 'moderate learning difficulties'. Senior members of staff in the two schools have been working to develop inclusive opportunities for both sets of students, and some have travelled between the schools to participate in lessons. As each school has a strong tradition in the area of performance art, this became the basis for a joint application to the government for specialist status and the schools were the first in the country to be awarded this as partners. They receive additional funding and are permitted to select up to 10 per cent of their students for 'aptitude' in performing arts.

The school is situated off a very busy main road leading to the city centre. There is a drive leading to the school, which is set in its own grounds. The school is modern-looking and compact, with no outbuildings. Entering it, you are immediately in a large foyer which is cavernous and not all that welcoming; the reception desk is at the far end. However, the school has used this space well. Around the large foyer there are displays of photographs and art work, reflecting the school's specialist arts' status. Along the walls there is an exhibition of photographs of past students, with information about their journey since leaving the school. Some have become teachers, doctors and lawyers. Equal space is given to students who have gained success by following vocational rather than academic routes.

INTERVIEWS WITH THE THREE HEAD TEACHERS

The head teacher of the boys' school

The head teacher had been at the school for some years. He extended a welcome from behind a large desk. In the room were his own children's graduation photographs. What did he see as the advantages of single-sex education for boys?

'I shouldn't say this, as the head teacher, I suppose, of an all-boys school, but I would prefer mixed schools, if I'm honest with you, socially. I think, if it doesn't sound too outrageous, that girls can have a civilizing effect on the boys and they have a different approach to life which, certainly in the formative years, is more intellectual and organized and I think that would be a role model for the boys . . . If I'm honest with you . . . mixed schools is probably my ideal.'

But

'It can be daunting for some boys . . . and can make boys maybe go the other way, but if it's all boys, there's a common culture. . . . There is a common culture and, I think, in any organization, if you can develop a common culture, you get a lot done, you mobilize all sorts of resources. . . . There is – I don't know – a brotherhood, I suppose.'

In fact,

'I think in many ways the pendulum has swung the other way and it's boys now that are insecure in their futures. It's boys who witness, really, a change in the industrial and commercial infrastructure of this country and where life after education goes to, and it's the girls, really, I think, in many ways, who hold a lot of the cards and have a lot more access to a lot more career opportunities.'

Yet, without the girls, the boys' approach to learning is 'very macho and competitive, which you have to control and you have to challenge otherwise, as you see, it all becomes counterproductive'.

One way in which the school challenges its macho character is by 'softening' the environment – hence the flowers – and by encouraging more students to participate in creative arts subjects like dance, drama and textile design and extra-curricular activities, for example juggling and running a school newspaper. The Personal and Social Education curriculum addresses such topics as relationships, puberty and being fathers, which were often taught by female members of staff. However, there are no female senior teachers in the school, 'which is a shame'.

Also, despite the decline in employment for young men,

'We tend to channel the boys still to traditional roles in society, whereas, I suspect – I have no day-to-day evidence, but I suspect – that a mixed school might tend towards male nursing, tertiary industry, chef-ing, restaurants, hairdressing, which doesn't occur to them in an all-boys school, they probably wouldn't like to admit it in an all-boys school.'

Responding to a question about the impact of selection on the inclusiveness of local schools, the head teacher gave a detailed description of geography and pecking orders:

> 'There is no question [this] is a very odd area. We seem to have, you name any type of school and we seem to have it. . . . We have all-boys, all-girls, we have several [foundation schools] and we have a boys' grammar school just up the road, with whom we're going in for joint technology specialist status, by the way, so we work well with that school. There's also a girls' grammar school up there. . . . It's all here really, within a few square miles.
>
> 'There's no question that the grammar school, of course, gets the peak of the intellectual crop, obviously. There's a huge waiting list. I understand all of that. I also think that we come third in the pecking order after the [foundation] schools. Selection makes it difficult for us to attract our fair share of grammar-school protential.'

Citing a range of 9 per cent to 50 per cent for the level of GCSE A–C passes across the city's schools, the head teacher reflected that there were non-selective local authorities whose results were much better. But his students come from 'very socially-deprived areas', with 'some of the highest unemployment in Europe'.

The head teacher of the girls' school

The conversation with the head teacher of the girls' school took place in her office and we sat in easy chairs. After a career teaching both girls and boys, she was 'committed' to single-sex education for girls. First, because the opportunity for them to develop confidence, independence, self-esteem and self-expression was 'not possible in a mixed environment'. Second, because exam results in single-sex schools were 'up there' and so girls' schools were popular with parents and thirdly because their ethos was 'caring and 'secure'.

The lack of social interaction with boys was the only disadvantage mentioned by the head teacher, but she listed a number of activities in which her students mixed with those from other schools, including University of the First Age (UFA) summer schools and enrichment activities funded by the government's Excellence in Cities 'Gifted and Talented' scheme. She 'seized all opportunities' to promote an attitude of 'The sky's the limit' for her students, though she admitted that, in practice, 'not everyone gets the opportunity'. For example, only about forty students out of a total of more than 1,600 attend each year's UFA summer school.

Within the school, the gender imbalance was addressed in a number of ways: the discussion of relationships within the sex education curriculum, an awareness of both gender and ethnicity stereotypes across all subjects and the promotion of non-stereotypical career aspirations: 'I feel very strongly that what the school offers through building the girls' self-esteem means that the low aspirations they may have had when they entered school are diminished.' She also argued that the social skills her students learned in school were about 'interacting with young people as a whole, not just young women'.

Of her approach to inclusion and exclusion, she said:

> 'It's a personal thing. I would feel positive [towards inclusion] wherever I was. Perhaps there are issues around the kind of caring and support, interpersonal issues that are more easily developed in a parallel environment . . . [girls] do much more easily collaborate, do look out for each other. . . . The predominant ethos of the school is towards inclusion and working towards including anyone who might be excluded in any sense. . . . I'd say it was typical of the school. . . . There is a very strong sense of mutual support, to the extent that one has to be careful it doesn't go too far . . . be careful you don't lose the rigour of ensuring that standards are maintained . . . firm and fair is what we try to be. If someone isn't conforming to what's required of them in the community, then that's dealt with. The first thought is to try and work through these things.'

Selection processes in the city do affect the school's community. But

> 'having said that, there are people within the neighbourhood who feel very strongly about comprehensive education and each year we get . . . parents who come along and say, "We're not entering our daughter for the selective exams". . . . 'So we do get girls who might have been successful if they had taken the exams.'

However, one or two students do leave at the end of Year 9, when they take the Common Entrance exam for entry into the independent sector and there is also a change for students at sixteen plus:

> 'Because we want access, post–sixteen, right across the city, we lose some of our girls to the sixth-form college . . . So does [an independent girls' school], so that creates vacancies there and parents still want [their daughters] to go there. . . . It's sad.'

The head teacher of the co-educational school

The head teacher of the co-educational school had been there for four years. Her spacious office was just off the foyer. We sat in easy chairs, and she asked for coffee. She held the same view of the differences between girls' and boys' approaches to learning and of the relative advantages of single-sex and co-education as the head teachers of the boys' and girls' schools: 'For girls, single-sex schools work, they're more motivated than boys. Boys are very competitive in the classroom and they have very different learning styles.' But: 'I strongly believe that mixed schools are best for all students, for their social development and for their future roles in society'.

However, there were some negative effects of the gender imbalance, for example in music and physical education: 'Because boys are more assertive in the way they approach practical subjects, they often monopolize the musical instruments.' Also, 'There might not be enough girls in the form or year groups to form teams that can enter for inter-school competitions.'

The head teacher wants the girls to feel safe and secure. In meetings of the school council, girls had expressed their feelings of vulnerability with so many boys around and they had asked for an area of the playground to be 'girls only'.

'They did not want an expanse of space to run around in but wanted quiet seating areas which would allow them some "time out" from the noise and bustle, where they could just sit and talk.' To ensure that girls are not disadvantaged 'it is school policy to ensure that girls are not isolated in groups, neither their form groups or their subject groups.' However, although intended to support the girls, this policy can also work to their disadvantage. Supporting the girls in a 'safe and secure learning environment' could 'compromise their academic potential': 'A girl could be moved up or down a group so she was not isolated, but the group that she moves into could be either higher or lower academically for her.'

The Personal, Social and Health Education curriculum offered assertiveness training for the girls, which the head teacher described as so successful that

> 'we decided not to leave it within this part of the curriculum, as some girls, if they are studying an extra language, do not have personal and social education, so we have extended it, so that all girls would receive this training.'

The head teacher then talked about changing the culture of learning for boys. She hopes that the school's specialist arts status will lead to a 'rounding of the edges' for the boys. This shift in emphasis, increasing the participation of boys in some areas of the curriculum, is also bound up with the extension of inclusive opportunities for the students of the partner special school. The head teacher describes this collaboration in terms of 'widening the outlooks' of the students from both schools.

Students' aspirations for the future are another concern of the head teacher. She feels that these are often based on cultural and gender stereotypes, which become evident when work experience is undertaken in Year 11 and particularly in the case of boys:

> 'Students are encouraged to find their own placements, but this just reinforces the gender stereotyping of work. This is going to be looked at

by the school in order to encourage students to choose alternatives, to challenge this limited outlook.'

This pattern is also reflected in the jobs students get if they go straight into work after school:

'They are sticking to traditional occupations, whereas if they go into further and higher education there is more variation and they make fewer stereotypical choices. This makes our display in the foyer so important. . . . We're having to do so much to counter the gender imbalance in the school.'

STUDENT PERSPECTIVES

We asked the students how they had made their choice of secondary school, what they thought about being in a single-sex or co-educational school and what changes they would make. One theme to emerge from their responses is that of the use of space. Students commented on the size of their schools, the quality of the environment and how easy or difficult it was to get around.

Students at the boys' school

Students in a Year 7 pastoral session gave us their views. The tutor, a PE teacher, made the class stand up as one of us entered the classroom. This impression of firm discipline was modified when he showed sensitivity in answering specific questions about the school and encouraged all the students to respond.

Why had the boys chosen this school?

'Because it was close to the junior school I went to.'

'I also came to this school because my friends go here.'

'Because it sounded good.'

'I chose this school because the male people in my family come here.'

A number commented on the quality of the education at the school:

'I chose this school because it had good high standards.'

'Because the school has a good reputation and it has high standards.'

'Because it has good results in exams and reputation.'

Several gave the absence of girls as a reason for the choice of school:

'So you don't see girls staring at us.'

'You can concentrate on work and not be distracted by girls.'

'You can talk about things you wouldn't talk about with girls.'

There was a general feeling that girls inhibited the way they worked at school:

'It's a lot more focused.'

'No moans from girls.'

'All girls keep talking.'

'No arguments from girls.'

However, when asked what were the disadvantages of being in an all-boys school, they said:

'There are more fights, boys argue more.'

'We don't get girls' opinion on a piece of work.'

'It feels funny without girls.'

'There's more messing around.'

'They tend to be more sensible and responsible.'

'It's boring having the same.'

Only one boy indicated that this school had not been his first choice: 'I didn't get into another school but I got into this school.'

Some students said that there were no drugs in this school and several referred to the school's strong line on bullying: 'It sorts bullies out,' 'It's good with the rules.' However, some also complained about the discipline, detentions and the uniform, specifically not being allowed to wear trainers. Students complained about the one-way circulation system in the corridors, saying that they wanted a two-way system, with proper banisters on the stairs. Outside, they would have liked a football field and other sporting facilities.

Students at the girls' school

Again, we spoke to a Year 7 group. Like the boys' group, the girls said they had chosen the school because their sisters had previously attended or were currently attending it, it was close to their homes and they had friends there. A number of the girls also said that their parents had chosen it because it was all-girls. The school's reputation was also important, for example: 'I chose this school, it is a girls' school and has good education. My sister came to this school, and when she gave her GCSE exams she had seven As and three Cs.'

They listed a number of advantages of going to a girls-only school:

'Girls take more care of you and know how you feel about certain things.'

'Not being teased.'

'Not as much arguing.'

'Not getting disturbed in your work.'

'Boys are unkind, and silly and do a lot of teasing.'

The disadvantages they saw included:

'We don't get boys' opinions on issues.'

'Can't learn to cooperate with boys in the area.'

'No opportunity to learn from boys and communicate with them.'

'The disadvantage of being an only-girls' school is that you can't have a laugh. Some of the girls are too serious or bossy.'

Most of the girls liked the idea of a big school, which made it possible to have a wide range of clubs, extra-curricular activities and opportunities for social interaction: 'You meet people from all over the world.'

As well as its being all-girls and having a large majority of Muslim pupils, the size of the school is a dominant feature:

'I would like there to be a shorter route from the centre to the upper and lower schools. I would also like there to be pathways in the big grass area, instead of having to walk all the way round.'

'We need more time at lunch. Everything takes ages.'

'I would change the canteen and make it bigger to fit us all in at a time.'

Among the changes that the girls would like are: lifts, a tuck shop outside the canteen, vending machines, to be allowed to eat outside, better toilets, a more efficient heating system, better equipment, a larger lower school hall, security cameras, personal lockers and showers.

Several girls spoke of bullying, especially from the older girls, but most of them said they had good relationships with teachers and dinner ladies. At the end of the day: 'Well, boys are on the other side of the gate, and when the bell's gone they try and come in.'

Students at the co-educational school

The views of students at the co-educational school were expressed at a meeting of the school council. Participants came from different year groups, and most of them were therefore older than those we spoke to at the single-sex schools. The students gave familiar reasons for choosing the school:

'My brother came here and liked it.'

'It's close to home.'

'A lot of my friends from primary school are here and some came with me.'

The students generally saw the advantages of being in a mixed school:

'We learn alongside each other, just as we did in primary school.'

'You can mix and meet more people and not always hate boys or girls.'

'You get to know how girls think about different things.'

They thought the separation for secondary schooling was 'nonsense'. Co-education gave them the 'opportunity to have friends of the opposite sex'. The boys felt that they were at a disadvantage because, as a result of boys being in the majority, the girls often did not get told off or punished for their behaviour. There are 'more boys than girls so what the girls do wrong is masked by the boys'.

The students felt they were listened to, however, and gave us two examples: 'We have been asked to say what we want the new school uniform to be like' and the girls mentioned their 'request for a seating area' in the playground. They agreed that there was not a lot of bullying in the school.

They were aware that specialist status had 'brought more money into the school' and that this meant that the school was 'very well equipped'. They were proud of this, though one student said: 'It has a lot of money but doesn't seem to want to spend it.' They did mention the links with their partner special school, but were not all that enthusiastic about working together:

'It means that sometimes we are in smaller classes.'

'We sometimes have teachers from the other school.'

'Sometimes we can't learn as well because they are slower.'

The students did not talk about 'inclusion' and there was a definite feeling of 'them and us'. It must be said, however, that the collaboration is new. When the students have had more contact, they will have more to say.

A parent's perspective

A Birmingham parent – who is also a local teacher – described the dilemma she faces in choosing a secondary school for her son:

'My own children go to Birmingham schools, and it's very very difficult to find . . . what you could call a true comprehensive school with a true comprehensive intake. The grammar schools affect that. . . . And single-sex schools as well cream off the girls. We've got on our doorstep a faith school, just set up. Hasn't had an impact on the intake of my school yet, but we don't know what will happen in the future. I mean, they're threatening to relocate nearer to our school so that may well have an impact, particularly on our girls. And at the moment I suppose our ratio of boys and girls is about sixty to forty, which is not bad really, given that there are single-sex schools in the area. . . . The set-up in Birmingham skews the ethnic intake and the gender intake. . . . Where I live, you've got the grammar schools, a [foundation] school is on the doorstep, you've got two girls' schools not far away, two boys' schools, the school my husband teaches at, which is a Catholic school, and they have been told they have to increase their Catholic intake and at the co-educational schools again we're very largely boys because the girls go off to the single-sex schools.

'I would love my son to go to a school with a truly comprehensive intake and I don't feel he can. . . . I would quite like my son to come to this school because I think the ethos of this school is good and we are a high-attaining school. But I know he would miss out culturally and socially, so it's a real problem. And, to be honest, I thought [the chief education officer] would have done something about it, but I guess his hands are tied because I know in grammar schools there's some kind of rule where you have to have a parental vote. . . . You don't know how his hands are tied really. It could be the influence that the government has now on deciding how many specialist schools there are going to be, and I don't know what could be done about it. I mean, it wouldn't be easy to say, "Right, we're going to get rid of this single-sex school and we're going to change its intake," and so on. I mean, historically, you're talking about these schools who have been here are well established and have been here for a number of years.'

DISCUSSION

These conversations with head teachers, students and a parent indicate that each of the three schools is shaped by gender stereotyping and by the effects of a variety of selection processes. In the all-boys' school, the macho culture was defended in terms of 'brotherhood' and there were no female senior teachers. Flowers and an extension of the arts curriculum indicate a 'softening' rather than a challenging of this 'common culture'. The views of the head teachers of all three schools imply that boys find it hard to concentrate in a 'civilized' atmosphere, that is, in the presence of girls. However, the boys themselves see the absence of girls as negative as well as positive and there are some apparent confusions, for example when they discuss, with a female teacher, what it means to be a father. In the girls' school and the co-educational school there is a further assumption: that the girls need safety, that boys are bound to make them feel unsafe. In the all-girls' environment, however, safety seems to be combined with a liberating rise in confidence. This school is more than twice the size of the co-educational school and nearly three times the size of the boys' school, confirming other evidence of the popularity of this combination of the traditional and progressive in single-sex girls' schools (see Ball and Gewirtz 1997).

The reasons given for single-sex education were different for boys and girls, as indicated by the higher expectations for the students' achievements and career prospects in the girls' school. The head teacher of the boys' school admitted that his students don't dare to move away from traditional occupations, even though the school is acutely aware that these are disappearing for young men and that, in confirmation of the study by Sally Power and her colleagues, this is a cause of real insecurity (Power *et al.* op. cit. p.152). Moreover, both students and parents at the boys' school said they had chosen the school because their results were good, when in fact it is not a high-achieving school because of the number of neighbouring schools that select by ability.

The ratio of boys to girls in the co-educational school is directly related to selection by gender, particularly into the large girls' school. This is also closely related to selection by faith, as most of the girls in the school come from Muslim families (see Chapter 5). For the single-sex schools, social interaction with the missing sex was an issue but one that was responded to with a range of outside-school activities. At the co-educational school, which should have enjoyed the social benefits derived from including both sexes, the three-to-one imbalance meant that interaction remained a problem and one that had to be dealt with in school. However, the school also sets students by ability. In the trade-off between ability and gender, in this school the otherness of being a girl determines her learning group.

It is not only teachers, however, who face dilemmas as a result of the highly selective nature of local provision. The right of parents to choose a secondary school for their son or daughter is seriously compromised (see also Chapter 4). If they choose a 'comprehensive' school, they are faced with the reality that, in the case of boys, they may be taught in boys-only classes and, in the case of girls, that they might be placed in a higher or lower ability group than suits them to prevent isolation from other girls. The schools that select by ability and the large girls' school all affect the intake of co-educational schools.

The ethos of a school, reflected for example in the expectations it has of its students, seems to vary according to the gender of single-sex settings. Compared to the boys' school, the girls' school appeared dynamic. Rather than the high-profile girls' school, it was the boys' school that appeared to be a refuge for its students. The girls' school was more active than the boys' in its pursuit of outside opportunities for the students to experience mixed groups. The head teacher of the girls' school referred to 'parallel environments', confirming the impression I received from all three schools that education and students' lives as a whole were seen as separate.

The head teacher of the boys' school imagined that students at a co-educational school would develop more flexible views about work and family life. This was consistent with the evidence from recent research (see Elwood and Gipps 1999) but not with what we learned about the co-educational school in our study. However, the head teacher of the co-educational school revealed that the Year 11 students, wherever possible, arranged their own work experience placements. This may have something to do with the perpetuation of stereotyped expectations and implies that there is an important role for the professional careers service.

The link between the co-educational school and the special school through a shared strength in performing arts is both inclusive and exclusive. Students from each school will increasingly work together, if not right across the curriculum, then in science and IT as well as the performing arts. Specialist status also brings the schools additional funding which is not available to other local schools. This scheme will eventually involve the co-location of the special school on the mainstream school's site and, perhaps, stimulate the beginning of a more thoroughgoing process of inclusion (see Chapter 4). The head teachers of both these schools are women. The boys' school is applying for joint technology specialist status with a single-sex boys' grammar school, indicating, perhaps, that the award of specialist status represents a change within the hierarchy of schools as well as a closer collaboration with a partner school.

The diversity of educational settings in this one small area of the city, with their varying levels of achievement and popularity, militates against comprehensive, community schooling. Though urban schools are being encouraged, through a number of government initiatives, to cooperate and share resources, in practice it is competition that is the dominant value. Processes of inclusion entail the erosion of barriers and categories. 'Mixed' gender, like 'mixed' marriage, may seem to be a kind of category mistake and, given current pressures to raise standards through selection and homogeneity, the 'looser boundaries' of co-educational schooling may not be valued as highly as the 'common culture' of a single-sex school.

CONCLUSIONS

We began with four questions: what impact does being in a single-sex school have on students' experiences; what do schools do to counteract their gender imbalances; what can they do to increase participation and reduce exclusionary pressures; and what criteria do families use in choosing a secondary school? It seems clear that the ethos of each school was noticeably different and that being single-sex or co-educational was a major determinant. The girls' school and the co-educational school were more actively engaged than the boys' school in activities related to the gender of their intakes. Each school was limited in what it, alone, was able to accomplish in terms of increased participation and reduced exclusionary pressures, though its individual policies definitely affected other local schools. They were operating within an elaborate system of which selection by gender was only one of the many layers. Families chose a school for a variety of reasons, including the expectation that an all-girls' school would do better than an all-boys' or a co-educational school.

The stereotype that single-sex is better for attainment and co-education better for social interaction remains widely believed in Birmingham, though it presents each of the schools discussed here with ongoing dilemmas and is not supported by the evidence of recent research. There does not seem to be an explicit critique of related factors, such as class, ability and faith, or a familiarity with recent literature, which could both show practitioners and families a more accurate and more complicated picture and support policy-makers to move with confidence towards greater inclusion. Selection by gender into single-sex schools reduces the capacity of all schools to develop as inclusive communities.

REFERENCES

Ball, S. J. and Gewirtz, S. (1997) 'Girls in the Education Market: Choice, Competition and Complexity', *Gender and Education* 9 (2): 207–222.

Elwood, J. and Gipps, C. (1999) *Review of Recent Research on the Achievement of Girls in Single-Sex Schools*, London: University of London Institute of Education, Perspectives on Education Policy, 5.

Gillborn, D. and Mirza, H.S. (2000) *Educational Inequality – Mapping 'Race', Class and Gender: A Synthesis of Research Evidence*, London: Office for Standards in Education.

Kenway, J., Willis, S., Blackmore, J. and Rennie, L. (1998) *Answering Back*, London: Routledge.

Kruse, A-M. (1996) 'Single-sex Settings: Pedagogies for Girls and Boys in Danish Schools', in Murphy, P. and Gipps, C. (eds) *Equity in the Classroom. Towards Effective Pedagogy for Girls and Boys*, London: Falmer Press and Paris: UNESCO Publishing.

Mahony, P. (1985) *Schools for the Boys? Co-education Reassessed*, London: Hutchinson.

Murphy, P. and Gipps, C. (1996) *Equity in the Classroom. Towards Effective Pedagogy for Girls and Boys*, London, Falmer and Paris: UNESCO Publishing.

Power, S., Whitty, G., Edwards, T. and Wigfall, V. (1998) 'Schoolboys and Schoolwork: Gender Identity and Academic Achievement', in *International Journal of Inclusive Education*, special issue on boys' underachievement, 135–153.

Smithers, A.Q. and Robinson, P. (1997) 'Co-education and Single-sex Schooling Revisited', Brunel University, Centre for Education and Employment Research (now at the University of Liverpool). [Also see Robinson, P. and Smithers, A. (1999) 'Should the Sexes be Separated for Education? – Comparisons of Single-sex and Co-educational Schools', *Research Papers in Education* 14 (1), 23–49].

Chapter 7

Student choice and participation in further education

Sharon Rustemier

INTRODUCTION

Student choice and participation are central to inclusive learning in further education (FE). However, the definition of inclusive learning which guides FE development pays insufficient attention to the social context of learning. While young people 'with learning difficulties and/or disabilities' are ostensibly included in mainstream colleges, their placement in these institutions is frequently on the margins, in discrete segregated classes. While such students are purportedly involved in college-wide processes and activities, they are often excluded in overt and covert ways. An examination of choice and participation for students on a pre-vocational programme in one college reveals processes of inclusion and exclusion operating on many levels, the social aspects of these processes having a profound effect on the experiences of the young men and women involved. What passes as inclusion can be seen in fact as a legitimized form of exclusion from what FE reputedly offers to all young people.

Introducing inclusion in FE

References by FE practitioners to 'inclusion' normally refer to 'inclusive learning', stemming from the publication in 1996 of the Tomlinson Report (FEFC 1996), taken forward through the 'inclusive learning quality initiative' between 1997 and 2001 and thereafter in the work of the Learning and Skills Council (LSC, 2001a, 2001b).

In this chapter I first define 'inclusive learning' and 'participation' as they apply to FE. I then introduce the college in which I investigate the experiences of students 'with learning difficulties and/or disabilities' and explore processes of inclusion and exclusion through studying students' involvement in curriculum decision-making and in cross-college surveys. In reflecting on these observations, I draw attention to a number of issues pertinent to developing inclusive learning in FE, for students generally and for those 'with learning difficulties and/or disabilities'.

A college of further education is a more complex organization than a school. There are students on part-time, full-time, daytime, evening, and distance courses. There are students on academic, vocational and recreational courses, aiming to enter higher education or employment or simply pursuing a personal interest. Some attend for a number of years; others for only a term. There is no upper age limit. There is no 'catchment' area. There is no national curriculum, although colleges do attract extra funding for courses aiming towards national targets. And there are no morning assemblies where all gather together in some semblance of unity. The point is that a college of further education is more heterogeneous than a school, so to take any one group of students, whether with the 'learning difficulties' label or not, would necessarily exclude others. However, in such a pluralistic set-up, this group is as legitimate as any other as a source of information about students' experiences. Through focusing on the students on the pre-vocational course I can probe in some detail the issues of inclusion which affect them.

Doing the research

The research was carried out during the 1997–8 academic year and took the form of four visits to Cropdot College plus correspondence and telephone conversations with key members of staff. During the visits I held formal and informal discussions with lecturers and programme managers, and spent one day attending sessions with a particular group of students. I attended an exhibition at the college, at which students' work was displayed and during which I was able to speak with staff, students, and representatives from local services in the city. I was also taken on a tour of the college and talked briefly with some mainstream lecturers and students.

Defining inclusion in FE

Inclusive learning in FE is theoretically concerned with all students. In practice it tends to be associated with those categorized as 'having learning difficulties and/or disabilities', probably a consequence of the Tomlinson Report being the work of the Learning Difficulties and/or Disabilities Committee of the Further Education Funding Council, the body responsible for post-sixteen education before it was replaced by the Learning and Skills Council in April 2001.

In discussing the Tomlinson Report, the chairman of the Committee, John Tomlinson, defines inclusive learning:

> Put simply, the concept the Committee have named 'inclusive learning' avoids locating the difficulty or deficit with the student and focuses instead upon the capacity of the teachers and the institutions to understand and respond to the individual learner's nature and requirements.

This means a move away from labelling the student towards creating the appropriate educational environment; to an emphasis on understanding better how people learn, so that they can better be helped to learn; and seeing people with disabilities and/or learning difficulties, first and foremost, as learners.

(Tomlinson 1997: 191)

The report emphasizes that students should be seen primarily as learners, predicating inclusive learning firmly on theories of learning and teaching, and on the identification of a student's 'learning style'. The influence of social and personal factors is acknowledged in that an analysis of teaching and learning should include: 'understanding the effects of an individual's cultural, social and personal experiences, including any disability or learning difficulty, on what and how they learn' (FEFC 1996: 32).

Essentially, though, inclusive learning is about matching the environment to individual student requirements. For Tomlinson (1997), this does not rule out segregated provision for some students, and he distinguishes clearly between inclusion as defined above and integration as the education of all students in mainstream classes. Despite some reminders that integration is an ultimate aim, the report's emphasis is on individual, not social, aspects of learning. It is not a matter of who learns alongside whom, but of matching the learning environment to the needs of the learning individual, whether this be in integrated or segregated provision. It is in this sense that an adherence to inclusive learning in FE can legitimize practices which would be undeniably segregative and exclusionary from a perspective on inclusion that values mainstream participation.

However, one frequently overlooked rationale for the conception of inclusive learning in the Tomlinson Report is the nature of the remit of the Committee:

to review the range and type of further education provision available, and to make recommendations as to how, *within the resources likely to be available to it*, the Further Education Funding Council can . . . best fulfil its responsibilities towards those students [i.e. with learning difficulties and/or disabilities].

(FEFC 1996: 203, my emphasis)

This appeal to resources is significant, not only in influencing what recommendations could realistically be made but in shaping the definition of inclusive learning itself. Evidently the report's inclusion/integration distinction, and the acceptance of segregated provision within the former, is strongly guided by resource considerations:

It is acknowledged that some groups or individuals consider that integration is the only acceptable objective, and have used 'inclusive' in this sense. The Committee were asked to advise how matters could be improved assuming only limited resources. Full integration implies a very well-resourced education system, if it is to do justice to all the students who would, as a matter of dogma, then always be taught in the same setting. The number of teachers and other experts that would need to be deployed, together with the range of technological help needed, would be more expensive than is now the case, where concentration of resources is achieved. Full integration as an aim should be retained and, when achieved, it will be coincident with inclusive learning. While we are working towards it, a more sound educational approach, in the view of the Committee, would be to match the resources we have to the learning styles and educational needs of the students.

(Tomlinson 1997: 193)

Pat Hood (1996) has argued that the resource-based nature of the report is a positive factor, its links with the funding body giving its recommendations more influence. Certainly, many have criticized those who promote inclusion without taking into account the realities of everyday life in FE, a reality which is increasingly resource-led (e.g. Lingard 1996; Barton and Corbett 1993). However, while funding will inevitably influence provision, there is a fundamental difference between resources influencing provision and resources informing the principles and philosophical aims underlying provision.

Defining participation in FE

'Participation' in FE is largely understood in terms of numbers of students on courses (e.g. Fairweather and Shaver 1990; Halpern *et al.* 1995; Kennedy 1997). However, meaningful participation is more than physical attendance (Potts 1992; Michailakis 1997). Indeed, Dee's (1997) examination of the fourteen-plus annual review process demonstrates that the involvement of students in decisions affecting them is frequently nominal. Tisdall (1996) similarly noted that a student's presence in post-school planning meetings gave the appearance of being involved, but in reality made little impact on the decision-making.

The definition of participation put forward by the Tomlinson Report incorporates both qualitative and quantitative elements:

There are . . . two dimensions to participation: the quality of provision of those who participate and the extent of participation itself. That is:
- ensuring that those already in colleges are enabled to take part more effectively in a learning experience which matches their individual requirements;
- increasing the opportunities for participation by those who are not currently participating in colleges.

(FEFC 1996: 53)

On both aspects, FE was found wanting:

> The volume of provision is probably meeting demand as currently expressed, but there is clear evidence that many groups are under-represented, including adults with mental health difficulties, young people with emotional and behavioural difficulties and people of all ages with profound and multiple difficulties. For those who are taking part, the quality of provision is not good enough, and as a result student experience is too often unacceptably inferior.
>
> (ibid. 10–11)

Whatever the extent of participation in FE measured in terms of numbers of students representing different sectors of the community, the exact nature of that participation must be examined if processes of inclusion and exclusion are to be revealed. As Booth (1996) states:

> The nature of a commitment to inclusion depends on how we define it. But we should not deduce too much from the few words that people give as their definition of inclusion. We need to know about the detail of their view of policies and practices concerned with participation in education.
>
> (p.91)

Exploring student choice and participation

Introducing Cropdot

At the time of the research, there were ten FE colleges in the city, although this situation is becoming increasingly complex with the government's emphasis on lifelong learning and reform of education for fourteen-to-nineteen-year-olds. Most of these colleges ran pre-vocational programmes for young men and women categorized as 'having learning difficulties and/or disabilities'. Until 'incorporation' in 1993, when colleges became self-governing and independent of LEA funding, many links were formed between colleges and schools that helped smooth the transition for these students. However, incorporation brought about more competition and less collaboration between colleges in recruiting these school leavers. Link schemes still operate between special schools and colleges, and between units within mainstream schools and colleges, but whether a student necessarily then attends that college or moves to another one in the city is less certain. The pre-vocational programme at Cropdot enrols many students who have attended link courses but also some from other schools in the city.

Cropdot is spread over four sites at the heart of the city, and attracts students with a wide range of cultural, ethnic and educational backgrounds. Until 1990, only higher-level courses were offered (NVQ Level 2 and above,

GCSEs, A levels and degrees). The employment of a manager specifically to deal with 'students with learning difficulties and/or disabilities' during that year met with some resistance: 'But we don't have learning difficulties here.' However, many students were identified as 'having learning difficulties' and were seen to benefit from the supported learning provided.

According to one middle manager, it was competition for students and falling standards that led the college to offer lower-level courses. GNVQ Foundation level is now offered in most curriculum areas, and provision for 'students with learning difficulties and/or disabilities' has grown. Nevertheless, the college continues to pride itself on the higher-level courses: after noting the various courses on offer and the progression routes possible, the course directory states: 'More importantly, around 400 people each year progress . . . to degree or other higher-level courses at universities' (my emphasis).

The discrete – i.e. separate, segregated – provision for students 'with learning difficulties and/or disabilities' is based not in a high-rise tower block like the mainstream provision but in a smaller building that was formerly a home for the elderly. It is from this building, officially called Barker House (unofficially 'Back o' Beyond'), that much of the college's inclusive learning work is coordinated.

In response to the Tomlinson Report, the college is collaborating with nine others in the region to examine quality assurance under the topic 'Design and Management of Organisational and Staff Development for Inclusive Learning', Cropdot's particular 'theme' being 'Collaborative work with colleges and other agencies'. In a cross-college briefing associated with this work, inclusiveness was defined as: 'an approach which promotes and supports the participation, progression and achievement of all potential learners, including those who are under-represented or who find access to, or learning itself, difficult'.

Stress is laid on the need for a whole-college approach: 'It is important to remember that Inclusive Learning is not just about making college life better for people with Learning Difficulties and Disabilities. It concerns establishing principles for a better learning environment for *all people*' (original emphasis)

What the staff say

Without exception, all members of staff referred to the Tomlinson Report when asked about their understanding of inclusive learning, though often with an implicit understanding of inclusion as meaning to go into the mainstream. For example, one manager noted that not all staff are fully behind inclusive learning, and there are those who teach on discrete provision who like the 'specialness' of it, not wanting to let go, saying, for instance, 'He won't cope out there.'

A programme manager of a course which caters for a wide range of students of all ages and levels of ability explained that inclusive learning 'means including as many people as you can in what you're doing . . . so in a sense [the programme] is an inclusive programme, though we don't work an awful lot with mainstream at the moment.' Another stated: 'It's all about widening participation and getting people in who wouldn't normally get in. . . . In fact, that should apply to all students, not just the ones with learning difficulties.'

And another:

> 'The definition we use is Tomlinson – making sure the environment is OK for every student so that all their needs are met and they can make the most of their learning opportunities. It's about providing sufficient and adequate support for every student, and the coordination of all that.'

However, this respondent pointed out that implementing inclusive learning is difficult because: 'different providers and organisations have different ideas about what it means to provide for each student, different expectations of what it means to meet students' needs'.

Social services want it to be a kind of 'normalization', she elaborated, treating each student as any other. In contrast, she explained, are the attitudes of a local organization for people with brain injuries and one for those with autism, both of which:

> 'are very aware of the differences in the needs of their clients and believe that they require a different service – the college has been criticised that the 'bog standard' support offered is insufficient . . . The [brain injuries organization] have called for different treatment of the clients and question the extent to which their needs can be met in mainstream classes. The Autistic Society have the same view and emphasize the special nature of autism. These different views and demands in turn encounter [the college department] which has its own idea of the level of support necessary.'

So while ostensibly the Tomlinson Report's acceptance of both integrated and segregated provision might be said scarcely to challenge what is offered to 'students with learning difficulties and/or disabilities', those who take seriously the notion of matching provision to individual student requirements encounter significant difficulties.

Investigating curriculum choice

The curriculum must be central to any consideration of inclusive learning. If students are seen primarily as learners, then the curriculum – the content and organization of what is learned, as well as the social relations of teaching and learning – is fundamental.

Student choice is also a key aspect of further education. One indicator of the 'adult status' towards which FE should be supporting students is 'the achievement of autonomy' (FEFC 1996: 7). Choice is particularly salient for those on pre-vocational programmes. For most students, the decision to study a particular programme is practically synonymous with the decision to attend the college: if a suitable programme is not available, then the student goes elsewhere. However, those on pre-vocational courses are often enrolled as a result of established school–college links rather than out of individual choice. Furthermore, they will be in college for x number of hours per week, and must choose enough options to fill those hours. This is a situation much more school-like than that faced by their peers and reflects an anomaly also recognized by Tisdall (1996): 'between, on the one hand, promoting disabled young people's independence and a successful transition to "adulthood" and, on the other hand, the frequent lack of young people's involvement in planning their post-school futures' (p.17).

Thus it is particularly important to maximize the degree of choice young people can exercise in order to minimize the effects of these social differences.

Cropdot College offers a variety of vocational and academic courses and various modes of study. Prospective students apply to the college's central admissions unit for a course of their choice and are then invited to discuss their application with a member of staff. This is followed by the offer of a place or guidance 'into an appropriate alternative' (course directory), by an invitation to attend enrolment and finally, for successful students, full induction onto the course. All students apply in this way, although this may be a formality for those whose enrolment results from school–college links. Those requiring support for their studies may attend a further additional support interview and/or diagnostic testing session.

The provision for students 'with learning difficulties and/or disabilities' is co-ordinated by a department which also supports ESOL (English as a second language) learners and adult basic skills. This department has been particularly successful in mainstream support of students with autism and Asperger's syndrome.

The department offers a number of discrete programmes for students from mainstream schools, special schools and day centres. In addition, courses are run in external venues, particularly in mental health outreach programmes – for example, a bicycle maintenance business – and for people suffering from brain injuries. A programme of jewellery-making is offered at a centre for disabled Asian women outside the college.

The pre-vocational experience

Students on the pre-GNVQ programme, aged between sixteen and nineteen, are allocated to particular tutor groups (eight students per tutor) but follow individual timetables, comprising fifteen one-hour sessions per week. In addition to the core skills of English, maths and information technology (IT), students choose from a variety of vocational and 'life-skill' courses, each accredited through the Open College Network and certified through the Record of Achievement. These curriculum options were increased substantially at the start of the 1997/8 academic year, and in preparation for dealing with this choice students were given training for decision-making. This included thirty taster programmes during the summer 'so that those with a learning difficulty could make more informed choices before enrolment'. All programmes were suspended in the fourth week of the term while individual students were invited to discuss their choices and review them where necessary.

The process of choosing options involved individual meetings between review tutors and each student. Most students were given their first or second choice of subjects. Although there were official limits to group numbers, in practice student preferences were accommodated flexibly. The order in which students were invited to make choices was opportunistic: existing students in June, new students in September, others 'as and when'. Preliminary indications are that this freedom of choice for students has been associated with greater retention rates.

The exercise has not been unproblematic. Lecturers and middle management noted that some students struggle with the degree of independence required. For example, staff complained that students frequently 'got lost' between classes and students themselves told me that having to travel between sites often made them late for sessions. In addition, staff noted a lack of continuity and stability in the teaching of English, maths and IT and a need to set more constraints around these choices, such as fixing core skills in the timetable and working choices around them.

One tutor complained that with so many subjects on offer and each student pursuing a different timetable, there is no crossover time between sessions; people opt in and out 'when you really need more continuity'; there are too many reviews – for example, one student had to fill in seventeen course reviews; changing registers is problematic and break times and lunch times are too short – 'so the knock-on effect of having one-hour sessions is organizationally a nightmare'. A student who was part of this discussion acknowledged that the degree of choice was good but the sessions were a bit short.

The tutor also commented that it was difficult to know where a particular student was at any particular time 'so there are problems if a parent rings', already highlighting the discrepancy between the rhetoric of fostering the transition to adulthood for these students and the reality of perceiving them as children.

What the students say

The perspectives discussed in this section are based upon my observations and discussions with students during a day spent attending sessions with them. I attended four sessions, with four different lecturers/tutors. This schedule had been arranged by my colleagues at the college, to whom I had written in advance of my visit outlining my research interests.

Of the four teaching sessions I attended, two were 'as normal' while I sat as observer. One session on communication was designed so as to encourage the students to discuss issues of choice and participation, and their feelings about college, with an opportunity at the end for me to address the students directly. The final tutorial session was left unplanned and 'open' for me to lead a discussion with the students, though in the event I was unable to conduct the session in this way.

How much choice did the students feel they had had in negotiating their timetables and in what they were doing on the course? This question was put directly by the tutor to a group of five students during an oral communications session. Varying degrees of satisfaction were revealed. Nicola was very satisfied: she felt that all her subjects were 'OK' and she had chosen them by herself. At the other extreme, Mavina replied:

> 'I didn't have much choice on my timetable. They gave me a timetable for English and maths, which is what I wanted to do so I could catch up; and then they gave me another one with Finding Accommodation and stuff like that on it – I didn't have any choice. . . . [But] I don't need the other stuff to prepare for GCSEs.'

The difficulty in Mavina's case was not because she had begun the academic year very late – which may have been expected to restrict her choice – but due to her desire to focus exclusively on English and maths. The basic skills provision is aimed at 'adult' (i.e. post-nineteen) students. Those aged between sixteen and nineteen who want to improve their literacy and numeracy are enrolled onto the pre–GNVQ programme and thereby have to take a variety of vocational subjects as well as the core (basic) skills. Such young people thus end up on a 'learning difficulties course', becoming labelled by default, and again demonstrating the way in which students categorized as 'having learning difficulties and/or disabilities', while being encouraged to develop towards adulthood, are excluded from provision that is designed for adults. Mavina's case is a clear example of a failure to 'match' the learning goals of a student with the learning environment provided by the college, and in so doing also reinforcing her non-adult status.

Of the three young men in the group, one was happy with all but one of his subjects. Nineteen-year-old Gavin said:

'Mostly I had lots of choice. We had the first two weeks then we could change and I changed what I didn't like. But there are a couple I still do [that I don't like]. . . . I have to make up the time . . . but I'd prefer to do more English and maths. . . . I did ask, but they clashed with something else. . . . Also money skills – I want less of that. I live on my own and deal with my own money. I wanted to do percentages and fractions and cooking, but they clashed.'

There was a notable difference in the participation of some students between this oral communications session and the following group tutorial session with their review tutor. Ian, for example, believed he had had 'some choice, some not', stating that there were some subjects on his timetable he had never been happy with but had not said anything about until now. During the oral communications discussion, he also noted that he wanted to do more writing and to do cooking as a subject, but was 'too scared' to say anything to his review tutor: 'I don't like saying. She'll just say no, but [the lecturer] says there is a place for me.' Responding to encouragement from the communications tutor, Ian did in fact bring the matter up in his next session. He had been attending assertiveness training sessions, and this was clearly an achievement for him.

Observing a number of different sessions proved informative in allowing comparisons of the varying degrees of student participation. For example, the positive experiences of Ian related above contrast strongly with those in another session that afternoon in which he had been particularly disruptive. Here, Ian had interfered with other students attempting to work, sworn continually under his breath, and clearly resented having to focus on the curriculum and not on his own concerns. Again, at issue was Ian's ability to make his own choices:

Ian: Stupid, this lesson is. I'm going. Lesson's rubbish. I'm going to tell my key worker.
Lecturer: Do you want to leave now? I'd like you to contribute to the lesson or leave now.
Ian: Fuck this. Wish I didn't come back. I was forced to come back.
Another student: You weren't forced. It was your choice. Why don't you leave?
Ian: And get one of those stupid orange forms and a rollicking off [the tutor] afterwards? This lesson's boring.
Student: You can go and speak to [the tutor] because it's not satisfactory for anyone. [Ian leaves]

Clearly, while it is important that young people be given the opportunity to express their views and to inform decisions that affect them, it is also important for them to learn when it is appropriate to withhold their opinions.

What was notable in this instance, I felt, was that even in constraining Ian's behaviour, the tutor treated him with respect. There was no question that Ian had something to say, nor were overt attempts made to devalue him: it was simply that now was not the appropriate time for expressing his views: 'If you don't want to be here we're going to have to talk to [your personal tutor] but while you're here I want you to sit up and pay attention. . . . Everyone's entitled to their opinions.'

However, the injunction to discipline both Ian's body and his mental focus – to 'sit up and pay attention' – can be seen as part of a discourse of control particularly entrenched in school education and thus again belying the 'adult' rhetoric surrounding these young people (see Gore 1995; Rustemier 2002).

In the final session of the day I observed a much more extreme form of control over the students, one which not only undermined any conception of them as young adults but even portrayed them as non-persons, unable to hold their own opinions or speak for themselves. In this session, each time I addressed the students, the tutor replied 'on their behalf'. For example, I asked: 'Can you tell me what it's like on this course?' The tutor commented: 'As his review tutor, if I can answer that. . . . I should report that Ian has been into the mainstream once so is not in a rush to re-enter – are we, Ian?' Ian agreed, though this was contrary to the opinions he had expressed so strongly in an earlier session. Again, when I asked him about his subjects, the tutor explained: 'He's had positive experiences, but I feel that really the programme lets him down, not pitching high enough for his IQ – the mainstream level is appropriate but everything else is not – it's a big change from school.'

Ian actually believes that his assertiveness training has made him more confident, and that college has made him 'more independent, I can get out of the house more'. Clearly, however, the degree to which he feels able to speak out is influenced by his perception of the situation and of those with whom he is interacting. It is doubtful that Ian would have been able to assert his opinion in the way required of Gavin in informing that same tutor of his wish to drop housekeeping:

Gavin: I'm not getting what I want. . . . I don't need to be supervised in order to wipe down a table.

Tutor: I think you're being unfair – the lecturer is new, and temporary, and that was her first session with you – I think you should give the lecturer a chance.

Gavin: You can think that, but the first two weeks were cancelled, last week was awful, if I go this week that'll be four weeks wasted. I've arranged to go to maths instead.

Tutor: I think you're using it as an excuse to do something you'd prefer.

Gavin: I'm sorry you think that.

In exploring the ways in which learning is a result of social interaction and not just a matter of individual knowledge and skills, McDermott (1996) was struck in his observations by how the experience of one pupil varied in different situations, as was the case for Ian. The young boy who features in McDermott's analysis appeared competent in different ways in different situations, with verbal interaction with others playing a significant role:

> Our question about how to describe Adam turned into a question about how to describe the settings in which the different Adams could emerge ... about the details of the conversations that were made available for Adam's different displays of competence.
>
> (McDermott 1996: 279)

In my own observations, verbal interaction between Ian and the tutor similarly appeared to play a highly significant role in drawing out different 'displays' of Ian's ability to express himself, and thus in determining whether processes of inclusion or exclusion were operating.

Taking part in surveys

The notion of active participation operates on a number of timescales. There is the immediate here-and-now of the meeting or other activity, there is the extent to which this involvement affects the short-term future of that individual in his/her situation and there is the extent to which the views of that individual feed into long-term change in the institution. The last is where college surveys enter the picture. As part of quality assurance measures in a college, it is customary to survey students about their perceptions, as well as to monitor statistical measures of attendance, retention and progression.

However, in his introduction to the Report, Tomlinson recognizes that students 'with learning difficulties and/or disabilities' are often not given full consideration in matters of quality:

> The work seldom features in college-wide systems of strategic planning, quality assurance or data collection and analysis. Few questions are asked about the purpose or relevance of what students with learning difficulties and/or disabilities are being asked to learn. Monitoring and evaluation of students' achievements is less common in this work than elsewhere and managers often lack awareness or understanding of what is required.
>
> (FEFC 1996: 6)

It is Cropdot College rhetoric that all students be included in processes of feedback as part of developing quality of provision. The College Charter openly invites students to: 'let us know where you think we have been successful or pass on suggestions of where you think we can improve your [sic] service.'

The college's Code of Practice for Equal Opportunities notes the importance of monitoring and evaluation of provision: 'The information collected should be used regularly to adjust and change the recruitment, admissions, curriculum and assessment policies and practices as and when examples of discrimination are revealed.'

Involving the students

There are many ways in which student feedback is obtained at Cropdot, ranging from informal feedback on a day-to-day basis to formal but limited student representation on the Academic Board, Student Council and other committees. However, the main vehicle for systematic collection of the views of large numbers of students is the use of questionnaires. Particularly important are the Student Initial Survey, the Student Satisfaction Survey, and the Student Course Review.

Staff reported that students 'with learning difficulties and/or disabilities' are involved in college surveys. Questionnaires are completed individually and independently as far as possible, but otherwise are completed as a tutor group, with each student making his or her own copy. This inevitably means that dissenting voices are unheard.

One manager/lecturer explained that there are a number of problems in getting at students' views. Most staff working with the students are unhappy with the format of the questionnaires, which tend to be very 'wordy' and complicated. This problem with format is acknowledged by the person responsible for designing the questionnaires. She readily recognized that 'students with learning difficulties and/or disabilities' seemed to be under-represented in questionnaire returns, although this is improving (fifty such responses to the 1997/8 Initial Survey compared with only four the previous year). In a recent Retention Survey:

> The forms were sent out and they were asked to fill them in, and I think [the lecturers] felt the questionnaire was not appropriate for their students' needs. So they would have focused on, probably, ESOL [English as a Second Language] students. The ones we've got for this year, again we will have more, then it's like any survey that is done. You look at the students' survey and you'll find a very small proportion of the students [with learning difficulties and/or disabilities] filled it in to other [departments]. Because you have this problem that the questions have to be standard. But if somebody helps them with it then that spoils the exercise. So I think that's an issue. . . . So it would probably be better to do something like this, which is taped interviews and see what they thought. . . . But again, I don't know, we'd have to try it out, so I'm not sure.

In addition to maintaining the 'purity' of the questionnaire method by using standard questions filled in independently, one reason for not modifying the format is the cost involved in terms of resources and time, and modification of other college material is a higher priority.

This manager explained that modifying certain documents is difficult because of the need for specific statistical information. The nature of the information needed plays a large part in dictating format, and if simplified too much for some students then the information gathered will not be comparable. Yet it is also the case that when using ratings of, say, one to six, the sophistication with which a student on a degree course answers compared to that of an Intermediate GNVQ student may also not be comparable.

The issues for those working with 'students with learning difficulties and/or disabilities' are summarized in the following quotation from personal correspondence on the subject:

> 'The student satisfaction surveys are not mandatory. We are in a dilemma. Do we give them to all students, knowing, then, that we have to help some people to complete them, and so run the risk of influencing their responses? Or do we select only the more able students to give them to and thereby bias the sample? The third option is to write modified-type questionnaires ourselves, but then we can't prove parity with responses from mainstream. I think in practice, because of this dilemma which we know we can't resolve, we tend to give out questionnaires in a very ad hoc way.'

In fact, the methodological problems outlined above are issues pertaining to all students, not only those 'with learning difficulties and/or disabilities'. They are also criticisms which apply to survey research generally, and are not specifically to do with the adaptation of questionnaires for particular students. Whatever its format, a questionnaire can pre-empt issues that respondents might raise and so obtain a preconceived view of their perceptions which may or may not concur with actual student feeling. The questionnaire can provide large numerical data far removed from the very individual and contextualized experiences of respondents. The objectivity and impartiality which a questionnaire supposedly allows are in reality compounded by the influence of the researcher in its construction.

Staff at Cropdot College working with students 'with learning difficulties and/or disabilities' recognize that simplifying questionnaires only addresses difficulties in a superficial way: choice and feedback issues are not only a matter of communication, and it is not only the questionnaire format which might exclude the views of those students. For example, one manager questioned the degree of choice some students have in attending sessions in the first place. Students from day centres might only attend on a particular afternoon, and so have a very limited choice of sessions: feedback may be more related to this than to their actual learning experiences. Another problem concerns how to enable students to respond honestly when they need the support of another person in order to complete the questionnaire, the support in this college being provided by members of staff (rather than peers, or volunteers). Attempts to bring in other staff to help evaluation at the end of sessions have met with limited success.

The manager responsible for quality surveys appreciates the importance of looking at individual cases and of using qualitative methods. In a Retention Survey of full time A level students, a pilot study of in-depth discussions with thirty such students was conducted with a view to identifying the sorts of factors that might predispose some to 'dropping out'. The replies were paraphrased and tabulated, and provide a rich picture of why people come to the college and why they might leave. However, there was still a desire to support the interviews with large-scale questionnaire data, and an interesting corresponding distinction between 'discussion' and 'research':

> We did taped interviews with thirty students in May '96. We asked them a set of questions, it was about a forty-minute interview and as a result of that, we knew that was just a sample and we knew that we wanted to confirm what we thought was whether our theory was establishable by research. So we looked at it and, there are two types of student at [the college], those that work hard and do very well and those that don't, so two distinct groups, and when you read through the initial survey. . . . We sort of backed that up. So our first thoughts were correct. . . . I don't think the in-depth research does more than confirm what we found out from the in-depth discussions with thirty students.

Nevertheless, the value of the interviews was recognized and the short-term plan is to arrange half-hour interviews for all students.

Reflecting

Examination of student curriculum choice revealed that students differed in the degree of choice they perceived they had had in constructing their timetables, and there was no straightforward mapping between this perception of involvement and the outcome of the timetable negotiations. Gavin clearly accepted the fact that some of his choices were not possible because of 'clashes' without feeling that his views had been ignored, yet he was unwilling to compromise his position when his opinions were regarded as 'unfair' and as an 'excuse'. For Ian, on the other hand, it seemed that the important thing was being able to speak up for himself. After many months of assertiveness training he was finally able to say with which aspects of his timetable he was unhappy and was able to request a change of subject from a tutor who generated significant anxiety in him.

The case of the college surveys demonstrates that although systems exist that will facilitate participation by students 'with learning difficulties and/or disabilities', and although management have thought about this, the practice is much more ad hoc and problems of questionnaire format continue to be cited as a barrier to full participation as far as certain students are concerned.

Both situations raise a number of issues. First, there is the importance of training and preparation for active participation (see Cooper 1993; Tisdall 1996). As Jenkinson has noted, the extent to which people are able to make decisions is heavily influenced by 'perceptions of limited competence, the issue of who has control over choices, and organisational structures' (1993: 361). Ian obviously benefited from his assertiveness training, and Gavin appreciated the review week during which he was able to reflect on his decisions and make further changes to his timetable. With various forms of support students have been able to complete questionnaires – the real concerns here go beyond the format.

The observations also highlight the importance of interpersonal communication and analysis of the interaction between students and others. The Tomlinson Report's neglect of the social should not obscure the fact that if its recommendations for teaching and learning are to be implemented then the social relations between learners and between learners and teachers must be addressed. If students are really to be involved in quality assurance systems, then the social organization that currently excludes them from such systems must be confronted.

A third issue is the distinction between speaking out and effecting change, or making a difference to the process and/or the outcome. Being able to speak out, 'finding a voice', is crucial to any experience of active participation (Potts 1992). Indeed, it is fundamental to the development of assertiveness skills, or 'self-advocacy' (Miller and Keys 1996). Yet there is a difference between speaking out and being fully involved, between 'giving a voice' and 'empowerment' (Troyna 1994). In fact, some writers have criticized the emphasis on the former and its frequent restriction to the immediate situation. For example, Aspis (1997) believes that rather than concentrating on the use of self-advocacy for negotiating with individual people in power, such training should be directed at changing the institution's rules, at changing policy in the long run. Similarly, Tyne claims: 'A great deal of "consultation" happens, with little result other than minor choices within existing service-options.' (1994: 251)

Such claims both simplify the situation and undermine the achievements of students such as those discussed above. It is not simply a case of minor choices versus major changes. Minor choices in existing structures allow individuals spending only a limited amount of time in an educational institution some experience of autonomy. The timetable system is set up in a particular way, and students are offered options within that. Of course there are some restrictions in the choices allowed when the system is in place before anything can be offered. When employees' incomes, college marketing and the plans of students themselves depend on these systems, some predictability is desirable. It is probably through involvement in college surveys that real structural institutional change is possible, but that takes time, and students on a one-year programme are unlikely to reap any benefits from their involvement.

SUMMARY AND CONCLUSIONS

So in terms of processes of inclusion and exclusion, what can be deduced from the experiences of young men and women on the pre-vocational course? On one level, there is the extent to which students are actually included in the systems that exist at the moment. This was discussed in relation to their timetable choices, which revealed that while the system was such that young people should be actively involved and included in decision-making about their own timetables, in practice there were occasions when individuals felt excluded from this process. Similarly within existing structures, the patterns of interaction between lecturers and students can have a powerful impact on the extent to which young men and women are included or excluded from everyday decision-making.

On another level, the system that faced these students in terms of timetable negotiation itself actually excluded them from what was happening in the mainstream of the college. The proactive efforts to give students experience of decision-making also in effect excluded them from the main body of the college, preserving their school experiences and child status. Under the guise of 'opting in' to FE life, students were effectively segregated from their peers. The perpetuation of a school culture whereby students are obliged to attend for a certain number of hours per week – even if that means taking a subject they dislike, makes their situation very different from that faced by their mainstream peers. One effect of this difference for the students concerned is the way it militates against the rhetoric of transition to adulthood and the development of autonomy that is the stated purpose of their provision.

The example of college surveys similarly demonstrates the danger of exclusionary practice resulting from a lack of active inclusive practice. When students categorized as 'having learning difficulties and/or disabilities' are not included in college surveys, they are being excluded from the whole process of student feedback. The rhetoric is inclusive; the reality is exclusive. The rhetoric refers to all as valued students, such that 'students with learning difficulties and/or disabilities' are included in the call for expressing their opinions, in developing to adulthood, in participating fully in the life of the college; but the reality is that many are excluded from participating.

Inclusion is about all students. Both student–tutor interaction and training for participation are likely to be salient to the experiences of students throughout the college. However, focusing on this one group has also high-lighted issues distinctive to these particular students, issues which arise directly from grouping these students according to their perceived learning difficulty/disability, i.e. perpetuation of the school culture, omission from college surveys, and age discrimination with regard to basic skills classes. Then there are those problems of questionnaire design that are erroneously assumed to be peculiar to these students. If inclusion and participation are really about all students, then both shared and distinctive experiences between any groups or individuals must be open to scrutiny.

In conclusion, then, this case study has illuminated a number of issues that must be addressed if FE colleges are to become inclusive. The fact that the very concept of inclusive learning seems to allow for both integrated and segregated provision should not obscure the fact that processes of inclusion and exclusion operate on many levels. To be included also means to have a voice, to be able to choose what, when and where to study, and to be studying for one's own reasons on one's own career/life path – all of which are questionable in the experiences of those with the 'learning difficulties and/or disabilities' label. Unless we take an inclusive approach to FE itself, that is, unless we refuse to exclude any aspect of FE from rigorous examination, then the pursuit of inclusive learning will remain a rhetoric and not a reality.

REFERENCES

Aspis, S. (1997) 'Self-advocacy for People with Learning Difficulties: Does It Have a Future?' *Disability and Society* 12 (4): 647–654.

Barton, L. and Corbett, J. (1993) 'Special Needs in Further Education: The Challenge of Inclusive Provision', *European Journal of Special Needs Education* 8 (1): 14–21.

Booth, T. (1996) 'A Perspective on Inclusion from England', *Cambridge Journal of Education* 26 (1): 87–99.

Chaiklin, S. and Lave, J. (eds) (1996) *Understanding Practice: Perspectives on Activity and Context*, Cambridge: Cambridge University Press.

Cooper, P. (1993) 'Learning from Pupils' Perspectives', *British Journal of Special Education* 20 (4): 129–133.

Dee, L. (1997) 'Whose Decision? Factors Affecting the Decision-making Process at 14+ for Students with Learning Difficulties and/or Disabilities', Interim Report presented at BERA Conference.

Fairweather, J.S. and Shaver, D.M. (1990) 'A Troubled Future? Participation in Post-secondary Education by Youths with Disabilities', *Journal of Higher Education* 61 (3): 332–348.

FEFC (1996) Inclusive Learning, *Report of the Learning Difficulties and/or Disabilities Committee*, Coventry: FEFC.

Gore, J.M. (1995) 'On the Continuity of Power Relations in Pedagogy', *International Studies in the Sociology of Education* 5 (2): 165–188.

Halpern, A.S. *et al.* (1995) 'Predicting Participation in Postsecondary Education for School Leavers with Disabilities', *Exceptional Children* 62 (2): 151–164.

Hood, P. (1996) 'How Important is "Inclusive Learning"?', NIACE briefing, Leicester: NIACE.

Jenkinson, J.C. (1993) 'Who Shall Decide? The Relevance of Theory and Research to Decision-making by People with an Intellectual Disability', *Disability, Handicap and Society* 8 (4): 361–375.

Kennedy, H. (1997) *Learning Works: Widening Participation in Further Education*, Coventry: FEFC.

Lindsay, G. (1997) 'Values, Rights and Dilemmas', *British Journal of Special Education* 24 (2): 55–59.

Lingard, Tony (1996) 'Why Our Theoretical Models of Integration Are Inhibiting Effective Innovation', *Emotional and Behavioural Difficulties* 1 (2): 39–45.

LSC (2001a) *Learning and Skills Council National Equality and Diversity Strategy: Widening Participation and Promoting Inclusion, 2001–2004*, Coventry: Learning and Skills Council.

LSC (2001b) *Report from the Forum on Learning Difficulty and Disability*, Coventry: Learning and Skills Council.

McDermott, R.P. (1996) 'The Acquisition of a Child by a Learning Disability', in Chaiklin, S. and Lave, J. (eds) (1996) *Understanding Practice*: 269–305.

Michailakis, D. (1997) 'When Opportunity is the Thing to be Equalised', *Disability and Society* 12 (1): 17–30.

Miller, A.B. and Keys, C.B. (1996) 'Awareness, Action, and Collaboration: How the Self-Advocacy Movement is Empowering for Persons with Developmental Disabilities', *Mental Retardation* 34 (5): 312–319.

Potts, P. (1992) 'Introduction' to Mason, Micheline *et al.*, 'Finding a Voice' in Booth, T. *et al.* (eds) (1992) *Learning For All 1: Curricula for Diversity in Education*, London: Routledge/Open University), 304–316.

Rustemier, S. (2000) 'Listening for Inclusion in Further Education', paper presented at ISEC Conference, University of Manchester, July 2000.

Rustemier, S. (2002) 'Inclusion in Further Education: The Experiences of Young People Designated "Students with Learning Difficulties and/or Disabilities", 1997–2000', Ph.D. thesis, Canterbury Christ Church University College.

Tisdall, E.K.M. (1996) 'Are Young Disabled People Being Sufficiently Involved in their Post-school Planning? Case Studies of Scotland's Future Needs Assessment and Ontario's Educational–Vocational Meetings', *European Journal of Special Needs Education* 11 (1): 17–32.

Tomlinson, J. (1997) 'Inclusive Learning: the Report of the Committee of Enquiry into the Postschool Education of Those with Learning Difficulties and/or Disabilities, in England, 1996', *European Journal of Special Needs Education* 12 (3): 184–196.

Troyna, B. (1994) 'Blind Faith? Empowerment and Educational Research', *International Studies in Sociology of Education* 4 (1): 3–24.

Tyne, A. (1994) 'Taking Responsibility and Giving Power', *Disability and Society* 9 (2): 249–254.

Chapter 8

A 'turbulent' city
Mobility and social inclusion

Patricia Potts

INTRODUCTION

On Monday morning, thousands of children and young people swarm round the city to study outside their home communities. They are going to schools that select their students: independent schools and grammar schools and special schools and faith schools and single-sex schools. They are travelling from the inner to the outer city and from the outer city to the suburban countryside. They are also moving home and school, over and over again, sometimes within one small area. Further, demographic and economic changes mean that some areas do not have a school at all. Someone I know called this 'musical schools'.

People on the move arouse deep-rooted feelings in those who stay put. They can be feared or envied. 'They' could be a threat to 'us', especially if our identity is based on a real or imagined place that is geographically fixed. However, not everyone who moves around is seen as a problem; 'globe-trotting' is what successful people do, and they are rewarded for being mobile. So when and why are mobile learners seen as a problem and how can perceptions and policies become positive and constructive? This chapter addresses the following questions in relation to the mobility of learners in Birmingham:

1   Why do learners move around so much?
2   What is the effect of repeated interruptions to learning relationships and friendships on the possibilities for sustained participation?
3   What can be done to provide continuity, security and stability?
4   Is reducing mobility the answer?

After presenting some recent research on highly mobile learners, I outline the situation in Birmingham and go on to illustrate and discuss two approaches to supporting highly mobile children and their families. I introduce an area of the outer city in which these initiatives have been implemented before going on to discuss each scheme in turn. Responding appropriately to mobile learners may involve the mobilizing of education rather than the immobilizing of children and young people. In this chapter, I have used pseudonyms for people and places.

RESEARCH INTO THE EFFECTS OF MOBILITY ON LEARNERS AND SCHOOLS

A study of mobility in primary schools in six English local education authorities identified four main kinds of movement into and out of schools: international migration, internal migration, movement between educational institutions and changes of home. The researchers concluded:

> Pupil mobility per se has not been found to be detrimental to the quality of education a school can provide, nor is there any obvious reason why it should be. The problems arise where there are very high levels of mobility, especially where children have particular needs and difficulties.
> (Dobson *et al.* 2000: 103)

Factors that did make a difference to the attainment of mobile learners were: refugee status, communication problems, unemployed parents, experiences of violence, debt, avoiding drugs and crime, personal conflicts, family separation, inadequate housing and leaving a decaying environment. A clear picture emerges from this study of the effects of poverty on the educational experiences of mobile children. Attainment levels in schools attended by children of armed forces families were 'relatively high' (op. cit., p.12).

Schools were not only affected by the disruption of highly mobile populations and by the need to respond to the range of difficulties experienced by the children themselves but also by financial instability and inappropriate planning demands:

> Head teachers with fluctuating school rolls have to manage fluctuating budgets and uncertainty in terms of forward planning. Setting targets for school performance in tests two years ahead makes little sense where there is a high rate of pupil movement. . . . Performance tables which do not reflect the real achievements of high mobility schools cause constant demoralisation to teachers working under extreme pressure.
> (op. cit., 101 and 117–8)

Strong local authorities are vital for supporting highly mobile children: 'If it were to be proposed that LEAs should have further reduced functions or cease to exist, the implications would need to be carefully considered in relation to access and achievement of the most mobile and least advantaged' (op. cit., p.118).

The head teacher of one of the primary schools involved in this study sees the mobile children as having 'great big histories' (Wallace 2000: 10). Taking a positive, enquiring, attitude towards people whose experience is different to those who do not move also characterizes educational work with traveller children. The tradition of metalworking around Birmingham is one reason for the numbers of traveller families in the area, where many of the men originally worked as blacksmiths. The West Midlands Consortium Education Service for traveller children has produced materials based on the assumption that the travellers' way of life is a valid culture with a rich history. From their years of working with traveller families, members of the Consortium have learned, among other things: 'That it is possible to accommodate nomadic lifestyles within official services'. They also state that: 'There are considerable inconsistencies in the effect of different legal instruments. There does not seem to be a political will to look at this as a whole. We are left with a feeling that this reflects endemic prejudice' (McDonald and Thompson 1999: 7).

A report of work with travellers in Scotland also argues that the issue for this group of mobile families is cultural and that schools should examine their own cultures in order to understand the exclusionary pressures these young people face:

> We would argue that where teachers do not reflect on the behaviour of traveller pupils and the reasons underlying it, this becomes a 'devaluation' of gypsy–traveller pupils and contributes to exclusionary pressures which in some cases lead to disciplinary exclusion.
>
> (Lloyd and Norris 1998: 366)

Schools can be seen as 'enclosures' and travellers as people on the outside, dispossessed. The restlessness that traveller children may experience when faced with the expected norms of behaviour in schools reflects the tension between belonging and identity that people experience whoever they are. It may also be that the difficulty of responding to traveller learners in schools is due not to their physical mobility but to the cultural immobility of both travellers and schools. Despite the good intentions of staff in many schools, traveller learners often remain marginalized. This may be understood in terms of institutional power as well as a clash of cultures: 'We see the "power" of schools (power as productive of mainstream culture) in their inability as institutions to include diverse groups' (op. cit.: 369).

A recent Performance Innovation Unit discussion paper, which looks at factors influencing upward and downward mobility rather than at the merits of reducing instability, cites evidence that a more equitable society in terms of income levels would be more, not less, mobile and that the relationship between education and mobility is not straightforward:

> There is no statistically significant association between variations in relative rates of social mobility between industrialized countries and

differences in type of education system, level of educational participation or measures of educational opportunity. . . . Even when individuals' level of educational attainment is controlled for, a significant association between an individual's class origins and class destination remains.

(Aldridge 2001: 22–23)

To compensate for social disadvantage would require redistribution on a massive scale. For example, one American researcher estimates that 'it would be necessary to spend at least ten times as much per capita on the education of black children as white children to equalise future wage earnings' (op. cit.: 32).

The literature presents some major challenges to education authorities responsible for highly mobile learners. What is the situation in Birmingham, and what kinds of policies have been developed in response?

MOBILITY IN BIRMINGHAM

Worries about mobile children are not new in Birmingham. A hundred years ago, the anxiety was expressed in eugenic terms:

> There can be no doubt that many parents of feeble-minded children, belonging as they so often do to the street-hawker and irregularly employed class, are even more migratory than the rest of the town's populations. This is one of our most disheartening difficulties; for, unless the after-care association can establish permanent custodial homes it must always lose a large percentage of cases, and every case lost may mean . . . a future generation of feeble-minded children.
>
> (Pinsent 1903)

In Birmingham today, people talk about 'turbulence'. In the school year 1995–6, the rate at which children and young people moved into and out of schools in each ward of the city ranged from 11 per cent to 32 per cent. In one primary school we studied later the rate was 56 per cent. High mobility between schools was related to high mobility between homes, though in each of the eight most turbulent wards, the mobility rate between schools was the higher. In 1997 the Education Department commissioned a close study of pupil mobility in one of the most turbulent wards and held a conference, entitled 'Moving Targets', to disseminate and discuss the findings in relation to the city's aim of raising standards of attainment through school improvement.

The average turnover rate for schools across the city was around 18 per cent, but in the ward included in the city's research project it was 26 per cent, rising to 50 per cent in one primary school and the secondary school. The secondary school has since closed, thus creating more student movement around the city, away from students' home communities. Supporting the study of pupil mobility in six local authorities I discussed above, the Birmingham research report noted the financial instability caused by 'turbulence':

> Money is withdrawn if pupil numbers fall during the year and fluctuating school rolls make it very difficult for schools to plan for the future, organise classes and set achievement targets. . . . There are implications for how schools can be supported in managing mobility and for reviewing the operation of the [Local Management of Schools] formula, as it applies to these schools.
>
> (Birmingham City Council 1998)

One of the primary school head teachers who spoke at the conference said that the model for education, a nuclear family staying in one place as the children grow up, was no longer relevant and that mobility was part of life for everyone, for both positive and negative reasons. However, if pupil mobility in schools is seen as the result of negative factors, it is not surprising if responses are based on crisis management, holding exercises to reduce mobility. Yet encouraging people to stay put by choice is also a way to restore and sustain urban communities.

Estelle Morris, a Member of Parliament for a Birmingham constituency and at that time Undersecretary of State for Education, gave the keynote address at the 'Moving Targets' conference. A number of the points she made have not been supported by subsequent research. First, for example, she argued that target-setting would raise standards in schools. The literature shows that this is not an appropriate strategy for schools with highly mobile populations. Second, she also argued that 'enormous social and economic difficulties [are not] themselves excuses for poor performance', when the literature shows that poverty is a much stronger determinant of poor performance by mobile learners than mobility itself (see Dobson *et al.* 2000). Third, she predicted that specialist school status would help schools to share good practice across local communities, whereas a recent Office for Standards in Education report has shown that this does not happen (OFSTED 2001). (Also see Birmingham City Council 1998.)

The regeneration of communities is one approach to reducing negative instabilities, and I have discussed this briefly in Chapter 2. Here, I examine the work of two multi-agency initiatives: Birmingham's family support strategy and a small education action zone, looking at how they each operate within one area of the outer city.

Birchwood

Birchwood is an outer-city residential area, smaller than one political ward, consisting of 1930s low-rise streets and a 1960s estate that has some high-rise flats. In 1995–6 the average turnover rate between schools was just over 20 per cent and the turnover of housing was nearly 15 per cent. Birchwood is separated from other similar areas by allotments, a secondary school campus and a large cemetery. Both the inter-war and the post-war housing were showcased when they were first built, but now the area has a negative image.

More than 90 per cent of the people living in the 1930s houses are white, reflecting the families' history of moving out from the inner city and social and private housing is increasing (see Chapter 2). The boundaries between the two parts of the area are becoming more distinct:

> 'The turnover of stock within the catchment area is predominantly in the post-war stock, where you went earlier. Around there and the "T" blocks, that's where the major turnover of stock is. Where you came into the estate, which is predominantly where the houses are, on the right, there is very little turnover.'

> (senior housing officer)

According to a 1997 profile of the area: 'The maisonettes are unpopular and most of these are occupied by single women with children. The high mobility or intended mobility off the estate results in a lack of motivation from the women.'

In 1997, Birchwood had slightly more children per household and more than twice as many single-parent families than the averages for the ward and the city. About 50 per cent of adults were unemployed and more than 50 per cent of families did not have a car. The estate had few shops and no playground near the flats, but there was a coffee shop, a pub, a residents' club and a Children's Society base.

Because of the demographic changes in this part of the outer city, the local primary school for Birchwood is in the same ward but not in Birchwood itself. The school was opened in the 1930s and originally there were three: infant, junior and senior. The secondary school was closed more than twenty years ago and demolished in the mid 1990s to make way for a private housing estate which incorporated two blocks of housing association properties. The school's head teacher told me that these 'filled immediately' but that 'there was great difficulty' selling the houses: 'Now it's ninety-nine pounds down and you can move in.'

There is high mobility in the area around her school and a frustrated desire to leave. Parents say to her: 'We feel trapped. We can't get out, we can't get away.'

'Many of the mothers have escaped domestic violence. Many families are running away from debts, in the expectation that they will be written off if they disappear. Some families move on after only a few months.'

(head teacher)

'Drugs are playing a major part in the need for people to move on. It's because of the number of burglaries or the fact that we've got pushers and addicts harassing people. . . . There's the concern of families about their kids getting involved in that sort of stuff.'

(senior housing officer)

The housing department faces a difficult task:

'Most of the people who live in Birchwood will want to aspire to Heathside [in the same ward]. . . . That's where their families are from. . . . Most of the requests for transfers . . . I end up having to deal with because the staff cannot get those people moved into the Heathside area. We don't have any two-bedroom flats in Heathside at all, so if we want to move them from Birchwood, where quite a lot of the stock is two-bed, particularly young families needing to get nearer to parents or to family for support, it's just not achievable.'

(senior housing officer)

The housing officer made a connection between the experiences of home and school of young people in Birchwood:

'Those kids, how do we ever expect them to form relationships and to hold any relationship, be it now or in the future, when they're constantly on the move and the only people they have any real contact with are their immediate family and maybe their cousins, at the most, but if, particularly for some families, where they've moved all round the city to escape violence or whatever, or purely on the basis that we can't allocate them where they want to be and they end up somewhere they don't want to be, how do we ever expect them to build relationships, to understand different cultures, to understand that people are different, when they're never in any one spot to do it for any period of time? And then we think, why do marriages break down, why do, you know, adult relationships break down, why's there all this violence on the streets? It's because people don't know each other and don't interact with each other, do they?'

Kingsbridge Community Primary School

Kingsbridge Community Primary School is in another part of Heathside ward but was involved in the Birchwood Family Support Strategy pilot project because it takes Birchwood children. The school is on one of the 1930s estates of semi-detached brick houses. The head teacher described her school as a 'ribbon village', a long, single-storey string of 'open verandas, one of the open-air type of schools'. These spaces have now been enclosed and enlarged, with the incorporation of internal corridors into the classrooms. The infant and junior schools are linked and form a wide arc around a large but treacherous playground that had pits and bumps in its sloping tarmac surface. This was due for repair the following term.

The school, which is also a base for a number of other community activities, is two-form entry, with places for 420 children but the total on roll was 360. Three new children had arrived one day I was there. 'The numbers go up and down week by week. This year the turnover will be around 35 per cent' – head teacher. (This was up from 24 per cent two years earlier.)

The priorities for family support in this school were related to the youth of many parents. A refrain of the recent OFSTED report on the school had been that the basic skills of children in the school were below average. The head teacher agreed:

> 'Children are grunting, pointing, they're not speaking in more than two words, three words. They've got dummies in their pockets. . . . There are very young parents, with mobile earphones and their little radios plugged in, and they come with the children like that in the morning and they go with them like that in the afternoon.'

There is a parents' room at the school, in a community project building across the playground. As well as social activities, the project provides parents with an opportunity to develop their own literacy skills. But parental involvement is not well established:

> 'I have tried everything. Their attitude is, oh, that's it, they're at school now, we can go shopping, have a coffee. They tend not to see the need for them to be involved. . . . Their [the children's] attendance and punctuality are appalling. School is not a priority.'

The head teacher referred to 'our turn-off year', the sort of comment you might expect to hear from staff in a secondary school talking about their fifteen-year-olds. The head teacher was talking about children half that age:

> 'The children stop coming in with their parents once they get to Year 4. The parents are saying, "They're grown up enough to sort themselves out now." Parental support with reading also tends to stop at Year 4, the parents thinking: "If they haven't done it by now, they can't and that's that." Year 4 children are out on the streets at night longer. They have a very poor attitude.'

So she has made Year 4 the focus of an 'inclusion project' that was outlined in the School Development Plan and has applied for funding from the city's Education Department. Year 4 and the nursery are the current priorities for this school, and the head teacher has allocated her resources for learning support to reflect these commitments.

The head teacher told me that when she came to the school she was shocked at how much of her time was spent on tasks that were not directly educational. You can feel the frustration in her description of the young parents in her community. A teacher in another primary school where the turnover of children is also high shares this frustration:

> 'It puts tremendous pressure on staff and it puts tremendous pressure on children because the dynamics of the classroom are constantly changing. When a new child comes in they might be taking your friend away, mightn't they? Friendships are so important to children. So the ones starting are worried they're not going to make friends and the ones in the class, well, "Is this new person a threat to my little world here?" It's difficult for children to feel included if they don't know how long they are staying. . . . I've had some children who've stayed for a week. You set it all up and then they've gone. It's just totally wasted time, extremely frustrating.'

Family perspectives

I talked to two families whose children attend Kingsbridge School. I asked them about their experiences of moving round the city and how they thought this had affected the education of their children. Jane Weston had two girls and a boy, aged from seven to nine, from her first marriage; she and her husband Sean have one daughter, aged two, and Jane was expecting a baby in six months' time. Susan Ryan had three boys and a girl, aged from four to thirteen, from her first marriage; she and her husband Paul had a baby of nearly one and Paul had a boy and a girl, aged seven and nine, from his first marriage. His son lives with him and Susan and his daughter lives with her mother. The boy may go to live with his mother, too, but Paul wanted him to stay with them.

Jane and Sean Weston, now in their late twenties, have known each other since they were teenagers and Sean's brother is married to Jane's sister. They had been together for three years, during which time they had moved more than a dozen times. Why? Sean said: 'We're moving on. To find the right place. It's about having a plan. We had neighbourhood problems. All I do is argue with them at the housing office. There was better places going to immigrants.'

By 'neighbourhood problems' Sean meant the violent behaviour of Jane's first husband, which increased when she tried to leave him. The head teacher at Kingsbridge had told me that Jane had been to a special school for young people seen to 'have learning difficulties' and that the statutory agencies were worried that she would not be able to look after her children on her own. When she did leave her husband, there was a lengthy battle for the custody of her children, which had finally been resolved in her favour. Sean gave up work and moved in with Jane to prevent the children being taken into care. He described the custody proceedings and the multi-agency assessment, as 'a very negative experience. There were lots of different people. It was very difficult for the children. But we got through it.'

They told me that the children find it hard to relate to adults, which is compounded because of their frequent moves and consequent changes of school. The children had been given what appeared to be a rather confused message about avoiding adult men. Because of the behaviour of their father, the older children had been taught to avoid 'strangers' rather than their father. Yet, because of their moves, nearly all the adults they come into contact with are 'strangers'.

Jane's eldest daughter was almost ten and would be transferring to secondary school in eighteen months' time. This had been raised at a review meeting in the school on the day of my conversation with Jane and Sean. They want the school to set up introductory activities this year, but the professionals at the meeting said that contacts were made during Year 6 not Year 5. Sean said: 'This is a big move. She won't cooperate straight away. We've got to get it sorted out now.'

Susan and Paul Ryan were in their early thirties. They had just got married, though they had been living together for several years. They had moved around the city half a dozen times in the past three years, and when I asked why, as with Sean's account of Jane's experience, Susan told me that it was because of the violence of her first husband. At one point she had gone with her three older children to a refuge for battered women. However, she had been forced to return to live with her then husband for a while, as she was unable to get him to move out and the council would not pay a second rent for the same family.

> 'I'd be there now if he had left. It had four bedrooms and central heating. A room downstairs had been converted into a bedroom with a toilet for John, who has cerebral palsy, but very mildly. He has some problems walking but he can talk okay.'

Her eldest son had settled in well at secondary school, but Susan told me that the other two boys could be difficult:

> 'They're only nine months apart and they're very competitive. They're not streetwise, like Simon. They don't go to the shop on their own. I daren't let them play out. They have to stay in the back garden. They'd talk to anyone, though they shy away from men more than women.'

There was an incident at one of the boys' previous schools about which Susan remains bitter. She had told the staff there that she was the only person to pick up the children from school. One afternoon, her ex-husband arrived, drunk, and made an attempt to take the children off with him. This was a shock in itself. However, Susan said:

> 'They blamed me. They said they didn't want this sort of thing happening. As if I had known anything about it. Or could have stopped it. I lost interest after that. I didn't send the children in for a couple of weeks.'

Kingsbridge is not the nearest school to where Susan and Paul now live, but Susan said:

> 'Kingsbridge is the only school who cares. The others didn't want to know. They didn't care. . . . They didn't pick up that they had special needs sooner. They should have been picked up earlier. It's the starting all over again. There is a school nearer to where we live, but we're staying at Kingsbridge.'

However, there are some negative consequences of this decision, for since their last move the family had no designated social worker. Susan said: 'They should allocate me another.' A consequence of not having a social worker was that the children could no longer go to the kids' club after school every day: 'I paid for two days and social services paid for three. They won't pay now that I've moved areas, so the children can't go.'

Occasionally, the whole family – Susan, Paul, six children and two dogs – go for a day trip to Blackpool.

The Family Support Strategy

A joint City Council/Health Authority Family Support Strategy (FSS) was implemented in Birmingham in 1995, following an Audit Commission report that revealed a countrywide lack of collaboration between statutory agencies when it came to working with 'children in need' (Audit Commission 1994). The aim was to develop more responsive and coordinated statutory and voluntary services, with a particular focus on children under five. There were eight pilot areas, funded in the following way:

> Each group has access to a small budget from joint funding to enable them to develop some of the targets agreed by the [steering group] and those identified by the local groups as having particular relevance to their areas. The implementation of the Strategy relies not on additional resources but on changes to ways of working between agencies and the contractual tasks of key workers.
>
> (coordinator, FSS steering group)

The education officer who coordinated the FSS Steering Group of thirty-seven members from different agencies and council departments listed the aims as they were set out in 1997:

> To promote and encourage good parenting across the city; to improve cooperation between professionals in the statutory and voluntary sectors; to develop new and more positive relationships between agencies and the local community; to act as a voice for each area and as a vehicle through which needs and problems can be channelled.

Criteria for selecting the pilot areas combined elements of both sets: there should be a high proportion of families with children, children on the child protection register and a high turnover of housing.

The steering group coordinator described a situation in which the city's statutory services were increasingly in demand by families with young children and told me that the approach was 'holistic': 'The right input from a very early age . . . so that the children in the pilot areas would have a more common baseline with children in other areas.'

The Birchwood FSS pilot area

When I visited Birchwood the project had been operating for about three years. The chair of the FSS Group gave me some examples of their work.

Bringing services together where people live

As a way to establish better communication with families whose requirements were complex and for whom separated specialist services were not appropriate, the group was planning an all-purpose centre:

> We're hoping to be able to demolish part of the shopping centre . . . 'cos we just can't let it. The flats above it are very unpopular and what we aim to do is develop a multi-agency centre. . . . We want to pull the housing team out of the building you went into because they're only there of a morning now, 'cos it's not a good environment. . . . The [children's charity] are next door in a couple of flats, so we want to pull them out of there. We want the [local church group] to come out of the shopping centre. [A local] housing association have got, I think it's sixty-odd properties on the estate. They do a weekly surgery through our office. That's something we've established in the last twelve months. So we want them to be part of this multi-agency centre. . . . Again, family support hasn't led these, but it's been the connections that we've made. Hopefully, we'll have the health visitors working from there with their own room . . . and we're developing a community flat where we're going

to do all our consultations with health visitors and, hopefully, have the family planning clinic.

Establishing ownership

The people I talked to in Birchwood gave me a picture of the dilemma facing both residents and service providers: to regenerate the area and help people build more stable lives where they are or to encourage people's aspirations and help them get out. The head teacher of Kingsbridge School said: 'Those who want the best for their children move out.' The senior housing officer said:

> 'What I want to see . . . is that we as a local authority get into the schools and do more work with the kids about the sorts of services we provide, why local authority housing isn't their goal and why it shouldn't be. Because at some stage we'll be dealing with the helpless and hopeless almost. . . . It'll be those people that really have no alternatives and what we should be doing is empowering kids to think about what their alternatives are. Just because your parents have come from a council house background and, I mean, I come from that background, that isn't your route . . . you need to think about what the alternatives are . . . and involving them in the planning of the estate in terms of its regeneration.'

Changing housing allocation policies

Until recently, people could make as many requests for housing transfers as they liked and those on the priority waiting lists for public housing could be offered a property in any area of the city. This meant that some families were on the move every few weeks and possibly to a different area each time. Of course this might have been what some families wanted, but for most people it added further unwanted disruption. Allocation policies are now evolving which encourage greater stability and commitment to the estates. In one of the original Family Support Strategy (FSS) pilot areas, the housing department was developing a local lettings scheme:

> To ensure local people wanting to stay in the area had an increased chance of doing so. This would be done by holding back 50 per cent of houses that become empty and prioritising them for people with the highest priority on the transfer list who live locally, as opposed to letting them in order of priority city-wide. Pilots will be monitored to check that this is not discriminatory under the Council's Equal Opportunities policy.
> (FSS pilot group update, March 1998)

The senior housing officer and chair of the Birchwood FSS group was setting up a system to limit the number of requests for a transfer to three a year, and he wanted tenants to sign twelve-month contracts. He argued that there was evidence to suggest that after about a year people began to make friendships and develop a commitment to their area. He also wanted to move away from the value system that used to determine housing allocations: 'No man, no house'. The perception that a mother and her children did not qualify as a 'real family' had prevented young families from moving from a flat in an undesired area to a house in a desired area. Further, homeless families had been seen as 'undeserving' regardless of whether or not a house would actually meet their requirements.

Evaluating the project so far

The chair of the Birchwood FSS steering group said it was early days and there were problems to be overcome:

> 'The problem with Family Support from the outset has been about people's commitment and I wouldn't be unfair in saying . . . it's been driven by personalities rather than the fact that it's somebody's role, somebody's job. . . . There's been about six to eight of us involved in the Birchwood Group who've been, we're the doers as I call it, not the thinkers and the do-gooders. There's been a number of people round tables, not just in Birchwood but generally, who are full of rhetoric but not full of action, and what happened in Birchwood was that we got a bit fed up with that. I've got a coordinator from social services who's very much a doer and let's-cut-the-crap type. She was, like, let's get this thing moving . . . so we just said, "Right, enough's enough." We got a smaller group of people together and we've driven it. . . . I'd have to say that education is one of the areas where there hasn't been a real commitment in terms of the doers. They've sent people along who were told, "It's an add-on to your job and it is for all of us," and it's an add-on that's not been particularly welcome in some quarters.'

The FSS coordinator in the Education Department acknowledged these criticisms:

> 'With the best will in the world, these people are doing it as part [i.e. part-time], you know, Chairs, officers, have tried to make sure it's a priority of theirs within the City Council and health, so it's been seen as a priority for others. But it is difficult for some people who're working at an operational level with big caseloads to suddenly turn up to meetings and play a part.'

She also agreed with the Birchwood's FSS coordinator that policy development had often been haphazard and reliant on personalities: 'There was no conscious thought or planning. You might think there was a preconceived notion but it wasn't like that. It was more like an evolution.'

A second kind of problem for the FSS was to overcome the traditional autonomy of the more prestigious agencies, such as health services. The housing officer who was the chair of the Birchwood FSS Group gave me an example:

Housing officer: Family planning's a real example of where we don't talk to each other. A decision's been made in the last month or so to withdraw the family planning clinic from the Birchwood estate, without any discussion with the Family Support Group.

PP: Why?

Housing officer: It's not effective. There's a real issue about where it's situated. It's in the [children's charity] and basically it's in a room with all their jumble . . . Well, it's a good idea to have it on the estate, but the problem was there was nowhere good to put it. . . . You wouldn't put it into the housing offices because people don't want to come in there because the only time they come in is when they're in trouble or when they want to have a moan at us, so it's in the [children's charity] in a room with jumble so people haven't been using it. So what we've been talking about is putting it into a flat we've got empty for the next few months while we develop concierge systems for the estate. But somebody's already made the decision without any reference to me as the chair. It's happened somewhere within one of the health trusts. And here we are trying to help families with young children and we've withdrawn one of the things. . . . And so we've written a stinking letter to the health people. That sort of thing has got to stop. But it's taking a long time to break that down and say, 'Look, before you make those decisions, you talk.'

The Heathside Small Education Action Zone

Birmingham established six non-statutory Small Education Action Zones (SEAZs) between 1999 and 2001. Despite receiving about a quarter of the funding of the larger statutory EAZs, the idea was that the SEAZs could be more flexible because they would be more autonomous and less bureaucratic (see also Chapter 2). In Heathside, a group of schools (including Kingsbridge) had been meeting together as an informal cluster for a couple of years before the establishment of the SEAZ. The focus of the Zone is the local secondary school and its nine major feeder primaries (there were twenty-six feeders in all, as the catchment area of the secondary school was in practice much wider than that of the ward). Schools self-select to be involved in the SEAZ so there are some schools in the ward that are not in the Zone. The Zone coordinator admitted that there was some 'ill-feeling' in schools outside the zone but added that 'everyone knows everyone' and non-Zone schools can participate in zone activities, for example a new training course about play. She said: 'We work as a ward.' Each participating school has an SEAZ coordinator and representatives from all the Birmingham zones, large and small, meet together termly.

The Zone has two main aims: changing attitudes to education and raising standards of attainment in schools. The first aim is to be realized through increasing attendance and motivation, reducing mobility and developing 'family learning': 'Because people move around, it's very difficult to form relationships' (Zone coordinator).

If children move around a lot, it is hard for them to make and sustain friendships in school and, consequently, to feel at ease participating in school activities:

> 'Last year we worked in one school where the majority of the class were boys. But it had been a class where a lot of the children had moved in so they hadn't really been together, they hadn't developed the friendship groups and they found it difficult to work collaboratively. . . . They worked with one of our drama specialists and there's been a 47 per cent increase in their ability to work together, to work collaboratively. . . . I think it's about the children seeing themselves as learners and providing learning opportunities that fit their style.'
>
> (Zone coordinator)

Many of the children are moving around for serious reasons, but the Zone coordinator also gave me an example of an apparently trivial reason for moving schools:

> 'We had one instance where a school didn't allow children to have crisps at lunchtime. They were providing fruit for them at breaktime. And one parent didn't like that. Her children were to have crisps rather than fruit, so she upped and moved all the children to another school. . . . In order to mitigate against that we try to get similarity of ethos, so whichever school in the zone parents go to, the standards of behaviour expected, a lot of the policies, will be the same, so that people don't move for these sorts of reasons.'

If children come and go without notice at all times of the year, then this undermines the stability of the school as well as of the families. A school with empty places is seen as less desirable than one that is full. A popular school will therefore perpetuate a more stable environment than a less popular one. Further, schools which might, because of their stability, be seen to be most capable of supporting children who experience a lot of instability in their lives, may also be those which are the hardest for mobile children to get into. Those schools which are the most popular and in which the levels of attainment may be high for the area may also help children and young people to develop higher aspirations for themselves and thus fuel the mobility of moving away and up, a more permanent leaving than the horizontal round that many families experience.

Do the Zone schools ever exclude children? The Zone coordinator told me that 'all the schools regard themselves as inclusive settings' and that permanent exclusions were 'almost nil', though temporary exclusions 'still need working on'.

I asked the Zone coordinator what she saw as the positive effects of the system:

> 'One of the highlights, really, is the change in staff and children's attitudes. There's been a real buzz over the past year. Everyone knows about the zone and everyone in every school has been touched by it in some way. Having two zone teachers actually working in schools has been really beneficial to both the children and the teachers . . . I think . . . one of our things is to create a vision of zoneness and we really have that and people feel they can drop in here . . . people feel they can drop in, it's not hierarchical. Yesterday I was in a secondary school and I had a meeting with the deputy head, the English coordinator and one of the cooks, and another volunteer wanted to see me. . . . So it's very much everybody. The training for dinner supervisors, they say what they want and we put it on.'
>
> (Zone coordinator)

Ashfield Primary School

Ashfield Primary School is a member of the Heathside Small Education Action Zone but had not been involved in the Birchwood Family Support Strategy pilot project. Like Kingsbridge School, Ashfield was built in the 1930s, in a low-rise estate designed for people moving out of the city centre from run-down Victorian terraces. Reflecting the original population, the area is still predominantly white and working-class. The head teacher described the community as 'strong' but added that there was a negative side, in terms of attitudes towards people who were seen as different.

There are 500 children in the two-form-entry school, including thirty part-timers in the nursery. About 40 per cent of the children are entitled to free school meals and a similar proportion is on the 'special educational needs' register. The school had been awarded Beacon status by the government, the only school in the Zone group to have achieved this.

In the early 1980s two local secondary schools closed, so children from Ashfield had to leave the estate when they transferred. Now, they go on to about ten different secondaries. Less than 50 per cent go to the nearest school, which, after a refurbishment and redesignation as a community school, is now popular but mainly with students who travel out from inner-city areas where a secondary school has closed more recently. The community of this secondary school is noticeably different, much more diverse than the residential areas close by, and it remains unpopular with Heathside residents. However, Ashfield maintains links with the school, for example through staff exchanges and joint training.

The mobility of families close to Ashfield itself is low, but this is in the context of an ageing local population: another factor that leaves schools with empty places and makes it easy for parents to move their children when there are disputes with staff:

> 'Many schools are running at 70 per cent capacity. This encourages mobility because when schools are trying to establish routines and acceptable behaviour, if that becomes difficult for some children and families to cope with, they're up and off. . . . So part of the mobility is mobility within the estate . . . in a relatively small geographical area.'
>
> (Ashfield head teacher)

Domestic instability is a major reason for families moving home and school:

> 'There's been a huge breakdown, even in the twenty-odd years I have been on this estate . . . and children see an incredible number of role models, not all positive, in their house. . . . We're in a throwaway society. If we can throw away a video and a television away and a car away, then in fact you can throw relationships away . . . when life becomes difficult in any form then, up to a point, there's a culture that you can replace it with something else better.'
>
> (head teacher)

What about the stability of the school itself? The head teacher saw staff turnover as positive – 'new blood' – but this was in the context of a senior team that had been at the school for many years. He said: 'You need both.' However, he also said that, at Ashfield, the newly qualified teachers (NQTs) tend to stay on, indicating that the turnover of staff was minimal and that recruitment would not be a problem. In the city as a whole, recruitment is not as serious an issue as in other parts of the country.

I asked the head teacher how the award of Beacon status had affected his school's relationship with the community and other local schools. He said he had felt 'uncomfortable' about the award and that he doesn't make a thing of it locally. It was awarded for the quality of teaching and management and the progress of the children: 'A successful school in a poor area.' But he said, though it was 'irrelevant', to it, it had made a difference to people's perceptions. Perhaps this was the reason why 'Beacon schools rarely work with their immediate schools'. Another might be that the award comes from the government, not from the LEA. A third might be that the status brings with it additional resources.

Ashfield School is the only one in the SEAZ group to have Beacon status. It is also the only school to have a male head teacher. I asked him if there was any connection. He said that, so far from this being a case of men moving in on the women's world of primary education, the culture of education in Birmingham used to be much more male-dominated than it is now. When he had begun teaching in Heathside, nearly all the primary head teachers were men.

DISCUSSION

The largely informal projects of the early and mid 1990s have been superseded by more formalized organizations with dedicated personnel and funding, a shift that reflects the impetus given to policies for combating urban disadvantage by the new Labour Government elected in 1997 and a tighter focus on raising standards of educational attainment. Family support remains a live commitment in Birchwood but, though a named FSS group still exists, inter-agency projects are now undertaken through the Small Education Action Zone.

The multi-agency centre for Birchwood is still under discussion, but the plans for resident 'ownership' and the reform of the housing allocation policy have made definite progress. The Zone coordinator told me that people do want to stay in Birchwood now and that there are 'welcome packs' for those moving in. Plans for regenerating the 1960s estate have received funding from the fifth round of the Single Regeneration Budget allocations (see Matthews 2001: 84–5). However, both families I talked to had experienced inflexibility in the response of inter-agency groups to current concerns, for example transfer arrangements (from primary to secondary school) and securing continuity of funding between social services areas.

The Zone coordinator told me that a report by the local branch of a national children's charity showed that there were many more domestic (nearly all male) acts of violence in Heathside than people had realized. However, I could find no evidence of a city-wide strategy for reducing male violence nor of connections made between domestic violence and strategies for social inclusion.

Projects are aimed both at stimulating people's aspirations to move on/out/up and at encouraging them to become involved in regenerating their area and stay put. There is a tension between these two aims, but, for most people we talked to, the latter is seen as a necessary first step, dealing with the moving-because-of-a-crisis before people can move-to-take-up-an-opportunity. However, the advisor for the Birmingham Excellence in Cities partnership wanted to see projects that encouraged people to use the whole city (see Chapter 2). At the moment, many people who do not move feel 'trapped'. Their lives are immobile rather than stable. Is the sense of belonging fostered by the Small Education Action Zone more valuable to them than an extension of their horizons?

The two primary schools I have described are in the same Zone, and yet the 'turbulence' experienced by one school is about three times greater. Why is the other school calmer? Reinforcing cycles of empty places and local perceptions seem to polarize the schools on a continuum of stability–instability. Management styles and school ethos are also relevant. However, these factors may mean that the school with fewer empty places also becomes the school with less diversity, a stronger but narrower ethos. Further, the published literature and the city's own research project have stressed the financial instability that results from learners moving into and out of schools and make recommendations that funding mechanisms should be revised to reduce this.

CONCLUSIONS

Many primary-age children in Birmingham are highly mobile, and this is seen as a problem because there are clearly negative consequences for their sustained participation in education. They move for a number of compelling reasons as well as for some that may seem trivial but which may indicate more serious difficulties between families and authority figures. If the settled institution of a school is seen as the proper place to provide learning experiences, then participation in education will be connected to reducing the mobility of learners. However, their mobility may not be the most significant factor in the underachievement and devaluation of highly mobile learners. Poverty and cultural differences may be more powerful influences. If this is the case, then it makes sense to accept the mobility of some learners and adapt educational services in response, aiming for a continuity of teaching and learning relationships based not on a fixed classroom space but on a more flexible social commitment.

REFERENCES

Aldridge, S. (2001) 'Social Mobility: A Discussion Paper', London: Cabinet Office Performance and Innovation Unit (tel. 0207 276 1470).

Audit Commission (1994) *Seen but not heard*, London: Audit Commission.

Birmingham City Council (1998) 'Moving Targets', unpublished set of conference papers, Birmingham Education Department.

Dobson, J., Henthorne, K. and Lynas, Z. (2000) *Pupil Mobility in Schools. Final Report*, London: University College London, Geography Department, Migration Research Unit.

Lloyd, G. and Norris, C. (1998) 'From Difference to Deviance: The Exclusion of Gypsy-traveller Children from School in Scotland', *International Journal of Inclusive Education* 2(4): 359–369.

Matthews, H. (2001) *Children and Community Regeneration. Creating Better Neighbourhoods*, London: Save the Children.

McDonald, T. and Thompson, M. (1999) *Travelling. Information and Training Pack*, London: Save the Children for the West Midlands Consortium Education Service for Traveller Children (tel. 01902 714646).

Office for Standards in Education (OFSTED) (2001) *Specialist Schools: An Evaluation of Progress*, London: Office of Her Majesty's Chief Inspector of Schools.

Pinsent, E. (1903) 'On the Permanent Care of the Feeble-minded', *Lancet*, 21 (2).

Wallace, W. (2000) 'Just Passing Through', *Times Educational Supplement*, 13 October, 2000: 10–14.

Chapter 9

Community, diversity and inclusion

Patricia Potts

INTRODUCTION

In this chapter I summarize what we have learned about processes of inclusion and exclusion in Birmingham between 1993 and 2001 and draw out some implications for developing inclusive school communities. I discuss the relationship between urban and educational renewal and return to the interconnection between politics and ethics put forward by Tony Booth in Chapter 1. The city is committed to equality of opportunity, access to education and the valuing of all learners. The realization of these aims, however, has not been closely linked to developing schools as inclusive communities. Some of the barriers to greater participation are to be found in the history and cultures of this particular city; others are related to factors currently affecting English cities more generally.

CULTURES OF EDUCATION IN BIRMINGHAM

During our years in the city, many people testified that there had been a real and positive change in perceptions of the education service. However, we also observed that various initiatives aimed at greater inclusion were unsustainable. There seemed to be a number of reasons for the fragility of these projects. First of all, their underlying values were not clearly set out, the funding was often insecure and their informal structures collapsed. Second, we were told that, despite frequent cross-party cooperation in the elected City Council, there was no 'political will' to tackle certain kinds of educational inequality. Certain selective and specialized schools enjoy a high status in the city and were seen as the source of valuable expertise and therefore candidates to lead reform. Third, the widespread and serious social disadvantage experienced in Birmingham has led to projects aimed at shorter-term crisis management rather than at establishing longer-term processes of social inclusion.

However, given the legacy of a complex and many-layered education system and the numbers of learners, families, practitioners and policymakers involved, would shared values and a coherent set of policies be possible? The resistance to initial moves towards inclusion was so strong in the city that explicit debates with oppositional interest groups were subsequently avoided. Education officers developed a 'charm offensive' and worked with colleagues from specialized settings as they might use a 'dating agency', looking for willing partners (see Chapter 3).

The city's Education Department was restructured in the mid 1990s (see Chapter 2) and a new 'special educational needs' division was created, separate from the pre-existing advisory and support division (as well as from the later-established equalities division). While this reflected the higher priority given to the education of excluded groups of learners and increased statutory duties, it also reflected the size of the organization.

There have been some positive changes over the last decade. The morale of students and adults in the city's non-selective maintained schools has been boosted since the arrival of the present chief education officer, and other changes have led to increased participation, for example, the work on reducing exclusions and the establishing of networks of support across schools and community bases. Although only a proportion of learners have so far participated, Birmingham's University of the First Age is also a potential mechanism for inclusion. Overall, however, there has been little change in the pattern of provision (see Hamilton 2001, for a brief discussion of social justice in relation to individuals as distinct from whole populations or systems).

We heard a confusion of discourses in the city: 'special educational needs', 'school improvement', 'raising standards', 'equality of access', 'inclusion' and 'value for money'. They were related in different ways by different people, and in different ways by the same people, at different times. It was rare for individuals to make links between processes of inclusion and community comprehensive schooling. Not surprisingly, therefore, no policy for inclusive education went beyond draft stage during our years in the city. The deputy chief education officer was emphatic about that (see Chapter 3). The inclusion team has been re-designated the inclusion consultancy, which does not play a role in policy-making.

Draft policies for inclusion in Birmingham have so far always included a commitment to segregated special schools, indicating the dominance of the language of 'special educational needs' in the thinking of policymakers: 'Along with mainstream schools, special schools play an equal and critical role in the development of inclusion within Birmingham' (City of Birmingham Education Department 1998: 3; see also Chapter 2).

So is there a local education authority where a policy for inclusive education has gone beyond the draft stage? In 1996 Newham, in east London, published a 'mission statement' and a 'strategic aim':

The ultimate goal of Newham's Inclusive Education policy is to make it possible for every child, whatever special educational needs they may have, to attend their neighbourhood school and to have full access to the National Curriculum and to be able to participate in every aspect of mainstream life and achieve their full potential.

Newham Council believes that all children should have an equal opportunity to attend a mainstream school, to have access to a broad and balanced curriculum and to be included in all the activities of the school that are open to pupils of their age group. . . . The Council aims to secure this equal opportunity for every child by promoting and supporting the development of inclusive education within every mainstream school and by ensuring that every child is able to attend a mainstream school and receive appropriate support in respect of any special educational needs they may have.

(Newham Council Education Department, 1996: 3)

There are no institutional exceptions, and membership of the mainstream is not to be conditional. Newham is much smaller than Birmingham, but the population is just as diverse and the levels of poverty may be higher. Newham does not have an elaborate structure of private and selective provision, and education officers and practitioners have worked hard to achieve a shared value system on which to base their policies. There has been a 'political will'. Newham has closed two of its five original special schools, one more is no longer admitting full-time students, and there is a coordinated system of support in nine primary and five secondary schools. Learning support services are themselves integrated and are administered from a base in the community.

GEOGRAPHIES OF URBAN AND EDUCATIONAL RENEWAL

There are other reasons why it is difficult for the elected members and officers of local authorities to reach agreement. Tony Booth has argued in Chapter 1 that there needs to be a defined area for the development of coherent policies and sustainable practices, and this view has been supported by professionals in Birmingham as well as the findings of recent research. The head of the Birmingham exclusions unit argued for a city-wide approach to providing community education for young people who had been excluded from schools (see Chapter 3) and the authors of the study of pupil mobility discussed in Chapter 8 (Dobson *et al.* 2000) argued that an organization on the scale of a local education authority was the appropriate mechanism through which to stabilize the budgets of schools with highly mobile populations of learners.

An OFSTED report, *Improving City Schools*, confirmed the inequalities in funding between schools, while not advocating a stronger role for LEAs:

> There is significant variation in funding from school to school and from area to area. Schools serving disadvantaged populations receive some funding designed to recognise the demands made upon them, but the basis and size of such allocations vary. OFSTED's latest analysis shows, alarmingly, that the greater the level of disadvantage faced by schools the more marked the variation in their funding becomes . . . the report points to the need for greater consistency in the funding of schools.
>
> (OFSTED 2000: 39)

The OFSTED report concluded that schools should be less dependent on short-term grants and given more control over their own budgets. However, it does not seem obvious that this would lead to consistency and fairness in school funding. Central government has taken over the control of many functions of local education authorities, while the financial autonomy of schools has turned others into services that are sold on a commercial basis to individual purchasers. In Birmingham, the substantial group of private, voluntary-aided and foundation schools also weakens the capacity of the LEA to implement consistent policies. The future of LEAs in England and Wales is at present insecure. Yet arguments for their retention are linked to increasing the participation of students.

Instead of strengthening local authority boundaries, the government has chosen another geography through which to deliver its policies for educational and social reform: the 'zone'. In Birmingham, the Education Action Zones cover either one or two political wards (out of thirty-nine, see map on page 15) and there is a range of perspective on how far they can support processes of inclusion. We have heard that the delineation of a zone can generate positive feelings of belonging. We have also heard that people feel trapped. We have heard the argument that focusing inter-agency initiatives within a zone is a way to make life and learning more rewarding for local communities, but the approach of many projects can be seen as compensating people for their deficiencies. The aim of a zone is to break down barriers within its boundaries, but we have heard that what is needed is to break down barriers to using the city as a whole. Whatever your perspective, however, the zone is a defined area of responsibility, like the city-wide local authority.

Spaces between schools

Educators in Birmingham have encouraged us to view the education 'system' as including the spaces between educational institutions. Institutional settings may be rigid and enclosed spaces compared to the potential flexibility of community-based services and collaborative networks of schools and colleges. Using these spaces in new ways depends upon new ways of thinking about the provision of educational services. An example in Birmingham is the University of the First Age. Other examples include the ways in which information technology allows students to maintain a programme of activities from a variety of bases. One education officer I talked to had put in a bid for a 'virtual' education action zone, but this had not been successful. All these projects destabilize the traditional classroom.

However, the situation is not straightforward. Schools experience statutory pressures to compete, to define their identities more clearly. How far can they therefore contribute to or benefit from the osmosis implied by collaborative networks? How far will collaborative mechanisms and what were once known as 'off-site' provisions, support the participation of learners rather than confirm the isolation of those excluded by the institutions?

Learning from the margins

Our study of the ways in which learners are excluded from education in the city has helped us to describe the features of a more appropriate and inclusive approach. For example, spatial stability/immobility may not be as inclusive as flexible social relationships between learners and educators that could be sustained across different places and times. Learners could belong to a base that is fixed but which does not require full-time attendance. The Paddington Barge School in London operated in this way in the first half of the twentieth century. Children had a pigeonhole in a classroom they visited intermittently. They were set tasks to carry out when they were travelling on the Grand Union Canal . . . to Birmingham.

We also discovered that mobility and gender are not prime influences over students' levels of attainment. Poverty and perceptions of difference are more potent factors. Therefore, staying put or retaining single-sex schools do not seem to be the most appropriate strategies for raising attainment levels.

Urban renewal

Revitalizing Birmingham's education service and revitalizing the city itself have been central projects of the 1990s, and perceptions of both have become more positive. However, urban renewal has not been accompanied by a commitment to comprehensive community education. Instead, resources have been directed towards strengthening diversity between rather than within educational settings, though collaborative networks have been established. Demographic changes have also made it difficult to maintain secondary schools at the heart of every community. Projects for urban renewal and the participation of learners in their communities are detached.

In his report *Children and Community Regeneration*, Hugh Matthews uses the phrase 'landscapes of powerlessness' to describe the relationship between children and young people to their environments and argues for their disenfranchisement to be reversed:

> The time has come when we should no longer rely on a traditional social science approach, which observes children's lives and goes on to report to policy-makers in the hope that they will bring about change and an improvement in quality. What is needed now is a more radical approach, in which children themselves 'learn to reflect upon their own conditions, so that they can gradually begin to take greater responsibility in creating communities different from the ones they inherited' (Hart, 1995, p.41). . . . For children, not involving them reinforces a sense of powerlessness and alienation. For adults, it establishes a positionality that further dislocates young people from their world. Fencing-off childhood in this way ensures that the hegemony of adulthood remains unchallenged on the landscape.
>
> (Matthews 2001: 73, 74)

According to this view, urban renewal is as much about communication systems and status relationships as it is about sums of money. The sight of children silenced by dummies and further cut off by their parents' headphones is a strong image of social exclusion. Communication between a young mother and child and between the family and the school has broken down. The story of parents taking their children away from school because of a row about crisps – although they stood up to the authority of the school – provides another example of communication failure. How far can regeneration projects empower these families to participate on their own terms?

Urban renewal has also been seen as a task of reversing the 'flight' of the middle classes out to the suburbs and commuter villages. The government's strategy for 'gifted and talented' students is an example of this. In his book *The Chosen City*, Nicholas Schoon (2001) provides a couple more. The first is a cash incentive, a council tax rebate scheme, and the second is what he calls a 'Fresh Start', in which communities of mixed housing and school building are designed and planned together. Education and housing cannot be separated, and regeneration has to include home-ownership. The assumption is that private sector finance is, directly or indirectly, necessary to the regeneration of inner-city education services.

However, as a recent article illustrates, when middle-class people move into a regenerated inner-city area, mixing is not necessarily what they want: 'A three-year study revealed middle-class "enclaves" had formed in these districts. Well-heeled "settlers" often sent their children to private or reputable state schools and shopped at upmarket delicatessens and specialist supermarkets outside the community' (Akbar 2001: 11). But the leading article in the *Independent* called these researchers 'the true inheritors of the coal-in-the-bath tendency' who live in the days when many people who did not like Mrs Thatcher forgot that all cities change and that London, with its long history of immigration from around Britain and the world, is one of the most dynamic.

(*Independent* 16 November 2001 p.3)

POLITICS, ETHICS AND DIVERSITY

Our studies of selection by attainment, faith and gender show that devaluation and exclusion is experienced throughout the city's education system. Parental and student choice is either frustrated by complex and inequitable procedures or else actively exercised in ways that perpetuate the disparities. Parental choice, described by the city's chief education officer as a 'virus' in Chapter 3, does not seem to be compatible with plans for neighbourhood renewal. On the contrary, it works to polarize the differences in social class, status, rewards and achievements of schools. Further, when schools are popular and full, selection procedures are reinforced. This is likely to be the case with 'specialist' schools.

A new policy for admission to secondary schools is under discussion in Birmingham at the moment, particularly designed to eliminate the holding of multiple places by families before making their final decision. Parents will have to state if they are making applications to private schools and the LEA will not circulate information about the rankings of their five permitted choices (increased from three). Criteria for entry into the city's 'community comprehensive' schools will be prioritized as follows: children in care, children identified as having 'special educational needs', children with siblings at the school and children who live the nearest.

Order and rationality

The head teacher of a boys' school in the city talked about the positive effect of the 'common culture' in his school. This is akin to having clear boundaries round a space or groups of people or a policy. It also implies that co-education is 'mixed' in ways that are not simply to do with including girls as well as boys but which are to do with the intelligibility of the project of education in that setting. The chair of the city's Education Committee defined inclusion in terms of comprehensive schooling. I would argue that the evident rejection of that view is the result of epistemological, as well as political and ethical, objections.

In a large city there is pressure to sort things out, to define clear boundaries, especially perhaps when the population is seen as under stress, insecure and disadvantaged. There is also pressure, in the current climate of educational values, to equate a good 'quality' education with specialist expertise, clearly defined targets, uniform assessment procedures and homogeneous groups of learners. All these pressures militate against diversity. How far the new work on 'citizenship' will further underline a 'common culture' for young people remains to be seen.

At the level of the LEA, there have been battles between the city and OFSTED over the clarity of educational boundaries, with Chris Woodhead, chief inspector until his resignation in 2000, reproaching the chief education officer for the muddled thinking of his plans for responding to students' individual learning styles. How could such a system be efficient?

The relocation projects between special and mainstream schools in Birmingham represent an attempt to break down geographical, pedagogical and emotional boundaries, even if they are also a response to falling rolls and impecunity. In one scheme each institution will retain a separate identity. However, the relocation may turn out to be a move towards a more equitable, less sharply defined, educational community (see Chapter 4).

We have found complexity, contradiction, tension and irresolution in the city's policies and practices. Even in the most controlled, classified and static system these would be unavoidable. A mature approach would be to accommodate complexities rather than strive to assimilate differences into an apparently uniform but still contradictory system. However, we have also argued for the value of working towards a coherent set of policies for inclusion, for which clarity and structure are basic necessities.

Diversity

Stability for learners can be associated with a strong school ethos, which may then be interpreted as 'consistency'. However, in areas of demographic homogeneity, poverty and instability (or demographic homogeneity, stability and wealth . . .), this can take the pressure off working towards a greater diversity of people and cultures. This may also be true for communities identified by one characteristic, such as gender or a particular faith, and we have observed hierarchies of provision across the city. Yet Birmingham is committed to diversity: 'The economic prosperity of the City and its social and moral climate depend upon the reality of social inclusion in a multi-ethnic, multi-faith community' (Birmingham City Council 1997: 6).

Increasing the participation of learners in comprehensive community provisions depends on the flexible crossing of boundaries, as well as the consistent implementation of policies derived from clearly expressed political and ethical commitments. Understanding inclusion in the city is an ongoing project, however, for the city is dynamic and elusive. In this book we have asked questions about the history and relative power of different inclusion agendas and, in evaluating the policies and practices in one particular city, we have arrived, here, with further questions. We have learned that competitive and exclusionary forces are strong. The capacity and desire of many schools to embrace diversity are underutilized.

REFERENCES

Akbar, A. (2001) 'Middle-class Settlers Fail to Join Community', *Independent*, 16.11.01., p.11).

Birmingham City Council Education Department (1997) *Strategy for Birmingham Towards The Year 2000*. Birmingham: Birmingham City Council.

Dobson, J., Henthorne, K. and Lynas, Z. (2000) *Pupil Mobility in Schools*, London: University College London, Geography Department, Migration Research Unit.

Hamilton, D. (2001) Foreword to Special Issue on Research into Education, Teacher Education and Social Justice, *International Journal of Inclusive Education* 5 (2/3) April–September: 97–101.

Matthews, H. (2001) *Children and Community Regeneration. Creating Better Neighbourhoods*, London: Save the Children.

Newham Council Education Department (1996) *Strategy for Inclusive Education 1996–2001*, London: Newham Council.

Office for Standards in Education (OFSTED) (2000) *Improving City Schools*, London: OFSTED.

Schoon, N. (2001) *The Chosen City*, London: Spon Press.

Index